Let's Chat About the Bible

Kingdom Kidz

Let's Chat About the Bible

Karen H. Whiting

Illustrated by
Eira Reeves

PROMISE
KIDS
AN IMPRINT OF
BARBOUR PUBLISHING

Contents

Dedication:

To my youngest son, Daniel.

Thanks for bringing joy to my life and for your excitement at chatting about the Bible with me.

Introduction

What would happen if your family turned off the TV, read, then talked about the greatest book ever–the Bible–for fifteen minutes some evening? That's what you are about to start doing with this book.

Adventure and Fun Talks Ahead

This is a Chat Bible. A chat is a friendly talk. With this Bible you get to do more than listen and learn. You get to talk about what you learn and whatever else the Bible makes you think about. You get to share your thoughts with your family!

You are a communicator. A communicator is someone who shares the truth, talks with others about what they learn, and helps others understand.

You and your family are about to take the most wonderful trip, or journey, in the world. You are going on a trip through the Bible.

Every journey goes better with a tour guide who makes sure that you discover the best people, places, and activities along the way. As you journey through God's Word, you'll have many different tour guides:

- *People who lived during Bible times.*
- *People who were there when adventures happened.*
- *People excited to help you learn more about God.*

Be an Explorer!

You and your family are explorers.
What does an explorer do?
you may wonder.

An explorer:
- *Travels to new places.*
- *Hunts for information.*
- *Checks out, or examines, everything he finds.*
- *Carefully questions, or investigates, the facts.*

Before leaving on a trip, people prepare, or get ready. They find out about where they are going and how to get there. They also make plans about what to do there.

Where are you going?

You are going through time to biblical places. The Bible is a record about God and what He and His people did over thousands of years. That's a long time, and it is a long journey. You will travel a little bit each day with this book.

Map of Israel

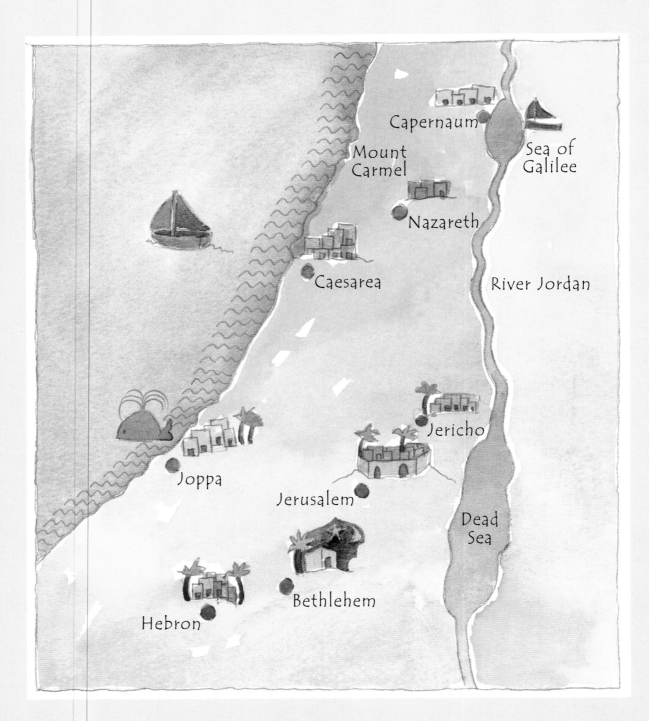

Most of the adventures took place in one small part of the earth in the Middle East called Israel.

Learning the Language

You will chat about special words. It helps you to understand people, and them to understand you, if you learn their language.

Signs to help you on your journey...

Time Tunnel

You and your family will journey through time and then go forward or backward through a time tunnel. When you are told to travel backward, go "Pow, pow, pow." When you are told to travel forward, go "Wop, wop, wop."

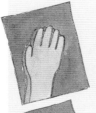

Prayer Time

Praise and prayer to the Lord.

Bible Time

A story from the Bible for you and your family to read.

Chat Time

Discuss the story you have just read and ask questions.

Journal Time

Write or draw about what you have heard, learned, or seen.

Get ready.

Gather your family so you can journey together. Choose the best time of day to travel and what days to travel.

Explorers record, or write down, and draw what they discover. You may want to bring journals, pencils, and crayons with you. After listening and chatting, you may write or draw about new things you learned.

Get set.

You need your ears, mind, heart, and mouth. You need to be polite in chatting. Let everyone have a turn to talk. Listen when others talk. Try letting the youngest children talk first.

A chat is friendly. Be ready to talk. Be happy when other people share what they think, even when it's not the same thing you think. If you don't agree, reread the words and see what God's Word really says.

If you want to talk longer, save some questions for the next day; that's okay. You are on a journey, not a race.

Now get going!

The adventure begins on the next page!

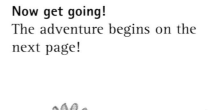

1 God's Creation

Bible Time Genesis 1-2

A long time ago God made the earth. Darkness covered the earth. It had no life. God knew He could make the world beautiful.

The earth needed light, so God said, "Let there be light." Light filled the earth and shone brightly. God called the light "day" and the dark "night." He made the first morning and evening. God was happy with what He created that first day.

The second day God chose to make something great–space. God made the colorful sky above the flowing blue waters. He liked it!

On day three God created more things. He gathered the water to let dry ground show. How clever! He called the dry ground "land" and the waters "seas." He looked and chose to brighten the earth. God said, "Let plants and fruit trees with seeds grow." Right then, bright-colored flowers, bushes, and tall and short trees grew. Brilliant color filled the earth! God looked and saw it was good.

Day four came, and God added special lights. He said, "Let there be lights in the sky to divide day and night and to divide time into days and years." God created a big, warm, round sun that shone brightly in the day. He made the moon with

I'm your guide, Noah.

You will learn about me later, when you read about a boat of animals, the first rain, and the rainbow. Let's explore the time before rainbows, before God made you or me.

- *Find out what God used to make things.*
- *Discover how God chose to make man different from all other creations.*

8

thousands of stars that twinkled at night. God saw it looked good.

On day five God decided to make moving creatures. He said, "Let swimming creatures fill the waters and flying birds fill the sky." As fast as God spoke, *splish*! *splash*! whales and all sorts of fish swam and dove through the waves, and colorful birds flapped their wings, flew in the sky, and sang beautiful tunes. The earth looked wonderful! God saw it was good, too.

On day six God added more. He said, "Let there be animals and crawly creatures." All kinds of animals came alive: big ones, little ones, furry ones, prickly ones, long-necked ones, crawly ones, and even some that swung from trees. . .all sizes, shapes, and colors. God had such fun! But, God wanted to make something special, more like Himself.

God said, "Let us make man in our image, like us, and let man be the leader on earth." God touched the dusty part of the earth, and out came man. When God breathed on the man, he came to life. God told him, "You are the leader on earth. Take care of everything I made: swimming creatures, flying creatures, and the animals and plants."

God saw that all He made was very good. God was so pleased! God blessed day seven as a day of rest.

Chat Word: *Create* is a special word. It means to bring into being or existence. Chat about the word *create* and how each person is creative.

Chat Time

Gather together as a family to ask and answer the following questions.
Have fun doing it!

Chat Word: *Creative* means to be good at thinking of new ideas or making things.

Have you looked at flower or fruit seeds? Do they look like the flower or the fruit?

How did God feel about what He made?
Talk about things you make and how you feel when you make something.

What does the word creative *mean?*
How are you creative?
What did God use to create things?
What can you do with words?

Did you find the time God used the word *very*?
When?
What was different?

What do you think it means to be made in God's image, like God?

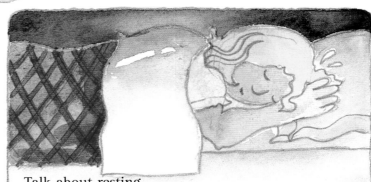

Talk about resting.
When is your best time to take a rest?
What do you enjoy when you take a rest?

Travel Time

Let's go forward through the time tunnel. *Wop, wop, wop!* The New Testament tells us a secret. It tells us the Word was there at creation, in the beginning. And it tells us the Word was God, and the Word became flesh. It became Jesus. Wow! You can find out about this in John 1:1, 3, 14 and Colossians 1:15-16.
How do you feel about the Word now?

Now let's go way forward through the time tunnel, past my time, past your time, to the end of earth's time. God will make a new, more wonderful earth. You can read about this in Revelation 22, the last chapter of the Bible.
How could the earth be more wonderful?

John 1:1 In the beginning was the Word, and the Word was with God, and the Word was God.

Journal Time

Write or draw about ways you can care for what God made.

Prayer Time

Dear God, thank You for having so much fun making things so that we may enjoy everything. Thank You for letting us look in wonder at the different skies, twinkling stars, the tall trees, colorful plants, and the land and sea. Thank You for making animals of all types and especially for making people. Help me care for everything You made. Amen.

2 The First Family Problems

Adam and Eve enjoyed life together as the first married couple. They lived in a beautiful garden God made called Eden, filled with fruit trees and a flowing river. How wonderful! But it didn't last long.

God gave this first family only one rule to follow. In the middle of the garden God planted two special trees, one called the tree of life, and one called the tree of knowledge of good and evil. God told man he could not eat from the tree of knowledge of good and evil. He could eat from all the other trees.

One day a tricky serpent asked Eve, "Did God really say, 'You must not eat from any tree in the garden'?"

Eve said, "Not from the tree in the middle. We can't even touch it, or we'll die."

The snake told her that the fruit would make her more like God. She looked at it, then ate a piece. She gave Adam a piece, and he ate it.

Hi again!
God made the first people and the first family. He gave them everything they needed. He didn't bring rain then. Mist wet the ground instead, something like the way dew wets the ground. Let's find out how this family lived. Let's explore God's Word and find out how the first family got along.

- *Listen carefully to the words of the snake and Eve.*
- *Find where the word "seed" is used.*
- *Discover how the first son hurt his own brother and why.*

We'll chat about these ideas later.

Then they saw they were naked and knew they had sinned. They tried hiding. This made God sad. He sent them out of the garden and told them they would have to work hard to grow food and have children. God made clothes for them from animal skins.

He cursed the snake and said Eve's seed would crush the snake's head, and the snake would strike His heel.

God used angels to keep people out of Eden. Adam and Eve left Eden and started a family. They named their first two sons Cain and Abel.

The boys grew. Abel took care of the animals, and Cain worked as a farmer.

One day Cain brought some fruits to offer God. Abel gave God his firstborn sheep. Abel's gift pleased God, but Cain's gift did not please God.

Cain became angry. God said, "Don't be angry. If you do what is right, I will like it. Do not sin."

Cain asked Abel to walk with him, and in the field Cain killed Abel.

God called out, "Cain, where is your brother?"

Cain replied, "Am I my brother's keeper?"

God said, "What did you do? Your brother's blood is crying to Me. You shed his blood."

God cursed Cain and told him when he tried to farm, nothing would grow anymore. He said Cain would have to wander the earth without a home. Cain cried and said, "But people will try to kill me."

God put a mark on Cain so no one would kill him. Cain sadly left his home and had his own family. Later, Adam and Eve had another son named Seth.

Chat Time

Chat Word: *Sin* means to do something wrong when you know the right thing to do. It is disobeying God. Talk about sin and how to not sin.

Talk about the words the snake and Eve spoke.

What did the snake use to trick Eve? Who was the snake?

Did Eve tell the truth to the snake?

Did God say they could not touch the tree?

What did God mean by the word seed?
Who were Adam and Eve's seed? Who else?

Chat about sin.

When you do something wrong, do you ever hide?

Do you ever try to change the rules or make them sound worse?

Have all parents, even yours, sinned? Can that help them understand you?

What happens when you disobey your parents?

Talk about families and problems.

Did Abel do anything to get Cain angry?

Did Abel notice that Cain felt angry or try to help Cain?

Have you ever felt so bad you wanted to hurt someone, even if they didn't hurt you?

Why do your brothers or sisters fight? What can they do to get along?

Travel Time

Let's go forward in the time tunnel to Luke 3:23-38. *Wop, wop, wop!* The Bible lists the ancestors of Jesus. He was a descendent of Adam. So Jesus is the seed of Adam and Eve. God had a plan for the birth of Jesus even on the day Adam and Eve sinned. **How did Jesus crush Satan?**

Luke 3:23-38 Now Jesus himself was about thirty years old when he began his ministry. He was the son, so it was thought, of Joseph, the son of Heli. . .the son of Enos, the son of Seth, the son of Adam, the son of God.

Journal Time

Write or draw about when your family had a good time together.

Prayer Time

Thank You, God, for making our family. Help us follow Your rules and get along. Thank You for sending Jesus to show us how to love each other. Amen.

3 Noah and the Great Flood

Bible Time Genesis 6-9

God saw the people He made doing wicked things. It broke His heart. He said, "I will wipe mankind from the face of the earth–men and animals–for I am grieved that I have made them."

But one man, Noah, found favor in God's eyes. Noah obeyed and walked with God. God told Noah He planned to destroy people. He told Noah to build an ark (that's a big boat), with many rooms in it. He gave directions for making the boat.

God said, "I will establish my covenant with you, and you will enter the ark." He added that He wanted to include Noah's wife and his sons and their wives. Noah did everything God commanded.

Whack, whack, whack and *bang, bang, bang* went Noah's tools as he built the ark. After he finished, God told him in seven days He would send rain to flood the earth.

What a busy week. In only seven days Noah filled the ark with animals, a male and female of every kind of animal and bird. Cock-a-doodle-dos, roars, honks, moos, quacks, and other sounds soon filled the ark. The animals came to Noah, for God sent them to the ark.

On his six hundredth birthday Noah entered the ark with his family. God shut the door. The storm began.

The ark tossed about as the springs of the earth burst forth with rushing water. Water poured from the sky. The boat floated high above the earth, on top of the waves.

For forty days and nights, splish, splash, the flood continued until the water covered even the high mountains. Every living creature and person outside the ark died. The rain stopped after forty days, but the earth stayed covered with water for many weeks.

Hello.

It's another great day to learn about God! Today you will hear my story–all about how God saved me from a great rainstorm and flood. Let's explore the time of the first rainbow and how it came to be in the sky.

- *Listen for how old I, Noah, was when I entered the ark.*
- *Find out why God sent a flood.*
- *Discover what I, Noah, did that pleased God.*
- *We'll chat about these ideas later.*

God remembered Noah and all the creatures in the ark. He dried up the waters, and the ark landed on top of Mount Ararat. Noah opened a window and sent out a dove. *Flap, flap, flap,* the dove flew everywhere but found no place to rest so *flap, flap, flap,* back he flew. A few weeks later Noah sent the dove out again, but the dove did not come back.

Noah waited a few more months until the earth dried up. God told Noah to release the animals. Everyone and every animal marched out.

Noah built an altar and made a sacrifice to God. That pleased God. God made a covenant. He said, "Never again will there be a flood to destroy the earth." God put a rainbow in the sky as a sign of the promise.

Chat Word: *Covenant* means "agreement." God and Noah made an agreement. God said He would not flood the whole earth again, and God asked Noah and his people to do some things, too. He told the people to have children, care for the animals, and not to murder other people.

Chat Time

Look at the water in the picture.
Can you see the land?
Why did God flood the earth?

Water cleans you.
Did God try to clean the earth with a flood?

THINK ABOUT THE FLOATING ZOO

How do you think Noah cared for the animals?
What animals do you see in the pictures?
What other animals do you think Noah put on the boat?

WATER

CHAT ABOUT AGE

How old was Noah? God used to let men live long lives. Read in Genesis 6:3, then talk about why God changed that.

84   100   600

NOAH PLEASED GOD

How did Noah please God?
Do you thank God?
How can you please God?

LOOK AT THE RAINBOW

God said when He sees the rainbow He remembers His promise. What do you think of when you see a rainbow?
Has God kept His promise?
Have men done what God told Noah to do?

Travel Time

Let's go forward through the time tunnel to the New Testament in the days when the Christian Church began, to Acts 22:16. *Wop, wop, wop!* Wow! Water is still an important thing to God, as part of *baptism*–something you do to obey God.

Acts 22:16 "And now what are you waiting for? Get up, be baptized and wash your sins away."

Journal Time

Draw a rainbow or write about a time you saw a rainbow.

Prayer Time

Thank You, God, for keeping Your promises. Help us obey You and please You. Amen.

4 Abraham Trusts God

Bible Time Genesis 11-22

God looked for a special person to help with the plans He had for the world. He found Abram, who lived in Haran, and told him to move away with his wife, Sarai. Abram obeyed. God promised to give Abram a child and multiply Abram's descendants. He promised to bless Abram and to bless all people on earth through Abram. What a big promise!

He moved to the land of Canaan with Sarai and his nephew Lot. Abram was seventy-five years old. They lived in tents and raised sheep and cattle. Abram waited many years. At eighty-five years old, Abram still had no children.

God spoke to Abram again. He said He would make Abram's family *sooo big!* He said, "Look at the stars. They are impossible to count. Your family will be much bigger." But nothing happened.

Abram tired of waiting for a son. Sarai told Abram to use her slave, Hagar, and have a baby. Abram did this, and Hagar gave birth to Ishmael. Abram loved Ishmael.

After Abram celebrated his ninety-ninth birthday, God spoke and made a covenant with Abram. He changed Abram's name to Abraham, which means "Father of many." He changed Sarai's name to Sarah, which means "princess." He promised that Sarah and Abraham would have a special baby boy.

Three visitors came to Abraham. Abraham fed them. They told Abraham that in one year Sarah would have a son. She hid and heard the talk. It made her giggle. Abraham was now one hundred, and she was eighty-nine. They were too old, she thought. But it happened. One year later Sarah gave birth to Isaac and felt so full of laughter. Isaac's name even means laughter. How wonderful!

But then God asked Abraham to do something strange. He asked Abraham to give up Isaac, to sacrifice him. Abraham loved Isaac, and he loved God, too. What a hard choice. Abraham trusted God and took Isaac to a mountain where he planned to sacrifice Isaac.

He laid Isaac on a pile of wood and prepared to set the wood on fire. At that moment an angel stopped Abraham, saying, "Do not do anything to Isaac. I know you fear God." Abraham proved he loved God, but they still needed a sacrifice. Abraham looked around. He saw a ram with its horns caught in a thicket. They used the ram and called the place "the Lord will provide."

Isaac grew up, and Abraham made sure Isaac married someone God chose. Sarah died, and Abraham married again. At 175 years old Abraham died. Ishmael and Isaac buried Abraham in a cave where Abraham had buried Sarah. God's plan began with Abraham. He had more planned for Abraham's son Isaac.

Hello, I'm Joseph.
Most people think of a beautiful coat of many colors when they think of me. That's just what I wore. It's what I did that you will learn about later. Today I want you to hear about a man who trusted God. He's my great-grandfather. Let's explore God's Word and find out about a man who lived in a tent and wanted very much to have a child.

- *Listen to what God promised Abram.*
- *Find out about a sacrifice God asked Abram to make.*
- *Discover the new names God gave Abram and his wife.*

We'll chat about these ideas later.

Chat Time

Chat Word: *Sacrifice* means to give up something you value. Talk about sacrifices you can offer to God.

God asked Abraham to move and give up his home.

Have you ever moved?

What do people give up when they move?

What did God ask Abraham to sacrifice?

What can you sacrifice?

MOVING

Many people move.

Have you moved or has a close friend moved away?

What was hard about it?

What did you learn from it?

WAITING

Abraham waited a long time for a son.

Have you ever waited a long time?

God answers prayer, but sometimes we need to wait.

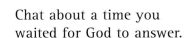

Chat about a time you waited for God to answer.

Travel Time

Let's travel forward in the time tunnel to John 3:16. *Wop, wop, wop!* God gave, or sacrificed, His only Son for us.
Talk about what that means.

John 3:16 For God so loved the world that he gave his one and only Son, that whoever believes in him shall not perish but have eternal life.

Journal Time

Write or draw about something you can give to God.

Prayer Time

Thank You, Father, for sacrificing Your Son to give us eternal life. Amen.

5 God Blesses Isaac

Abraham sent his servant to his brother's homeland, in Nahor, to find a wife for Isaac. He said God would help. The servant took ten camels to the city. He prayed for a sign from God to know who to choose.

He prayed that when he asked a girl for a drink she would say, "Drink and I will water your camels, too." Before the servant stopped praying, Rebekah came for water. He asked, "Please, give me a little water."

Rebekah gave him water and said she would water his camels, too. She was the granddaughter of Abraham's brother Nahor. Wow! God answered the prayer.

The servant met Rebekah's family. He told them about his journey to find Isaac a wife and his prayer. Rebekah's father, Bethuel, and her brother, Laban,

listened then said, "Take her." Rebekah agreed to leave right away. Isaac married Rebekah and loved her, but they had no children.

Isaac prayed, and Rebekah had twin sons, Jacob and Esau. These boys fought and pushed inside Rebekah. God told Rebekah that each boy would lead a nation, and the older would serve the younger one.

Hard times came with no water or food. It was a famine. Isaac moved to Gerar where God told Isaac to stay. He said He would bless Isaac as He blessed his father, Abraham. God promised to give the land to Isaac and to make his family *sooo big!* A family with as many people as the stars.

Isaac planted seeds. God blessed Isaac. Even in the famine the seeds sprouted and grew and grew. Isaac reaped one hundred times what he planted! Isaac became very, very rich. This made the Philistines who lived nearby unhappy. They filled up the wells Abraham's servants had dug. Their king said, "Move away. You are too strong for us." Isaac did not fight. He moved to the valley.

Isaac's servants dug new wells, but each time men in Gerar yelled, "That water is ours!" Isaac moved farther, and his servants dug another well. No one fought so Isaac named the well Rehoboth. That means "room," because Isaac found enough room for his family and servants. Again God said, "I will bless you."

Abimelech, the king of the Philistines, came to Isaac. Isaac asked why he came after being so mean. Abimelech said, "We saw that God blessed you, and we want peace." Isaac held a big party. At the party they promised each other to live in peace. That day Isaac's servants dug a new well and found water. Isaac named the well Shibah, which means "promise," and named the town Beersheba, which means "well of the promise." Isaac lived there for the rest of his life.

Hi again!
I hope you enjoyed learning about Abraham. Today you will learn about my grandfather, Isaac, and my grandmother, Rebekah. Let's explore God's Word and find out what God did for Isaac and why.

- *Listen for the names of the wells.*
- *Find out how the servant chose a wife for Isaac.*
- *Discover what happened when Isaac planted seeds.*

We'll chat about these ideas later.

Chat Time

Chat Word: *Blessings* are gifts from God. Chat about ways God blesses people.

Who really chose the wife for Isaac?
What did the servant pray?
How did Isaac feel about his wife?

Do you ever ask God to show you a sign for an important choice?
Who chose the people in your family?

What made the Philistines upset?

Do you ever get upset when someone does better than you?
What should you do when you are upset?
Why didn't Isaac fight?
When people were mean, what did Isaac do?
When the king finally wanted peace, what did Isaac do?

FOOTBALL

Do you try to make peace even if you have to give up something?

Travel Time

Let's travel forward to Mark 10:16, in the New Testament. *Wop, wop, wop!* We see Jesus and His disciples. Oooh, children are running to Jesus. Oh, no, the disciples won't let them get close to Jesus. Yea! Jesus says, "Let the children come." Jesus blesses the children. God can bless people, and since Jesus is God, He can bless people, too. **Chat about how Jesus wants to bless all God's children.**

Mark 10:16 And he [Jesus] took the children in his arms, put his hands on them, and blessed them.

Journal Time

Draw or write about how God has blessed you and your family.

Prayer Time

Thank You, Father, for blessing us. Help us to live in peace even when others are mean to us. Help other people see that God blesses us so that they may want to know God, too. Amen.

6 Jacob and Sons

Bible Time Genesis 25, 27-29, 30, 49

It's me, Joseph, again.
It's getting closer to my story. Today you'll learn about my father and my family as well as a little more about me. You already read that my grandfather, Isaac, and grandmother, Rebekah, had twin boys. Let's explore God's Word and find out about their son Jacob:

- *Listen to what God told Jacob.*
- *Find out how Jacob tricked people.*
- *Discover about someone who tricked Jacob.*

We'll chat about these ideas later.

Rebekah gave birth to twins. She named the hairy son Esau because that means hairy. His brother came out holding Esau's heel. She named him Jacob, which means "trick," or "grab a heel."

Esau hunted animals while Jacob was quiet and stayed home. Isaac loved Esau, but Rebekah loved Jacob. One day Esau came home and saw Jacob cooking stew. It smelled great. Esau said, "I'm starving, let me have some red stew." Jacob said, "Only if you sell me your birthright," meaning Esau would give up all land and money left when Isaac died. Esau agreed and ate.

Isaac grew old. He asked Esau to hunt and cook meat the way he liked it, and then he would bless him. Rebekah overheard and told Jacob to trick Isaac. She would cook meat Isaac's favorite way, and Jacob would pretend to be Esau. Jacob argued that the trick would upset Isaac, but Rebekah told Jacob to obey her.

She put goat skins on Jacob's arms to make him hairy. It worked. Isaac blessed Jacob. When Esau came home, Isaac found out about Jacob's trick but had no blessing left for Esau. This made Esau very angry, and he planned to kill Jacob, but Isaac sent Jacob away to Rebekah's brother, Laban.

On his journey, Jacob stopped to sleep. That night Jacob dreamed of angels going up and down a ladder to heaven, with God standing at the top.

God told Jacob He would make his family *sooo big!* with more people than the dust of the earth. He also promised good would come to all people through Jacob's family. He said, "I will be with you and watch you wherever you go."

Jacob awoke and went to Haran. He met Laban's daughter, Rachel, at a well, and she took him to her family. Jacob worked for Laban. Jacob said that instead of pay he would work for Rachel to be his wife. On the wedding night, after seven years of hard work, Laban tricked Jacob by sending his older daughter, Leah, to Jacob. Jacob worked seven more years to marry Rachel.

After many years, Jacob returned home, sent gifts to Esau, and made peace with him. One night on the way home Jacob fought an angel. At daybreak, the angel touched Jacob's hip and hurt it. Jacob asked the angel to bless him. The angel said he had fought men, and God and won. He blessed Jacob and changed Jacob's name to Israel, which means "God strives."

Jacob had twelve sons and one daughter. Each son became the head of a large tribe of people. He loved his first son born to Rachel the most and named him Joseph.

Chat Time

Chat Word: *Nation* means people sharing the same culture or government. Chat about your nation or the nation of Israel today.

JACOB'S FAMILY

Jacob tricked his brother and his father. Chat about that.

Who tricked Jacob? Is it good to trick someone? Is teasing like tricking someone?

GOD SPEAKS

Chat about how God spoke to Jacob in a dream and after a fight.

How does God speak to you and people in your family?

God promised Jacob a big family. Do you remember who else God said would have a big family? Are they all the same family?

FAMILY

Jacob's twelve sons became the heads of tribes of the nation of Israel. They did become a big family. God chose one son, Judah, to be the tribe from which Jesus was born. Talk about that.

How big is your family?

What do you know about your grandparents and their parents?

Travel Time

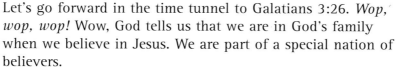

Let's go forward in the time tunnel to Galatians 3:26. *Wop, wop, wop!* Wow, God tells us that we are in God's family when we believe in Jesus. We are part of a special nation of believers.
Chat about what it means to be in God's family.

Galatians 3:26 You are all sons of God through faith in Christ Jesus.

Journal Time

Draw or write about your family tree or draw the faces of people in your family.

Prayer Time

Dearest Father, thank You for making us part of a big family, Your family. Forgive us if we have ever tricked anyone. Help us be good and kind to the people in our family. Amen.

7 Joseph, a Man Who Trusted in God's Plan

Bible Time Genesis 29, 37–48

Jacob loved his son Joseph the most. Jacob gave Joseph a beautiful coat of many colors. His brothers hated him.

Joseph told all his eleven brothers about his dreams. In one they tied piles of wheat in the field. Joseph's wheat stood tall, but all his brothers' wheat bowed down. In another dream Joseph saw the sun, moon, and eleven stars bow to him. His brothers hated him more.

One day Jacob sent Joseph to check on his brothers. They saw him coming and planned to kill him. One brother, Reuben, argued no, just throw him in a well. *Ripppp, rippp,* they tore off Joseph's coat and threw him in a well. They sold Joseph to men going to Egypt. Then they put goat's blood on Joseph's coat and told their dad a wild animal must have killed Joseph. Jacob cried for days.

In Egypt, the men sold Joseph as a slave to Potiphar, the captain of Pharaoh's guard. Pharaoh was the leader in Egypt. God blessed anything Joseph did. He ended up in charge of Potiphar's house.

Potiphar's wife tried to make Joseph sin, but he ran away. She lied and told Potiphar that Joseph tried to hurt her. Potiphar threw Joseph in jail!

Even in jail God blessed Joseph. The jail keeper put

Hello.

Today's story is so exciting because it's all about me, Joseph! Some of it seems sad, but it has a happy ending. Let's explore God's Word and find out how I ended up living far from my family.

- *Listen to what God meant for good even if people meant it for evil.*
- *Find out why my brothers were so mad at me.*
- *Discover how God used dreams in my life.*

We'll chat about all this later.

Joseph in charge of other prisoners. Two men thrown into jail had strange dreams. Joseph said God knew what the dreams meant.

Pharaoh's cupbearer dreamed about three branches of grapes. He squeezed the grapes and filled a cup that he gave to Pharaoh. Joseph said this meant in three days he would be freed and wait on Pharaoh again.

Pharaoh's baker dreamed three baskets of bread sat on his head. Birds ate the food from the top basket. Joseph said this meant that in three days Pharaoh would hang him.

All Joseph said came true. Two years later the cupbearer saw that something troubled Pharaoh. Pharaoh had a dream, but no one understood its meaning. The cupbearer told Pharaoh about Joseph, and Pharaoh sent for Joseph and said, "I heard that you can understand the meaning of people's dreams." Joseph said, "I cannot, but God will give the meaning of your dreams." Pharaoh learned that his dreams told of coming good years followed by years of hunger. Pharaoh put Joseph in charge of Egypt. Joseph stored food from the good years.

When years of famine came, Jacob sent his other sons to Egypt for food. Joseph knew them and forgave them. Joseph said, "You meant to harm me, but God meant it for good. God used it to deliver many lives." He had his brothers bring Jacob to Egypt, and they all lived together.

Chat Time

Chat Word: *Deliver* means to save. Talk about how God used Joseph to save lives and how Jesus saves lives.

FORGIVENESS

Joseph's brothers hated Joseph and did mean things to him, but Joseph forgave them.
Is it easy to forgive someone?

DREAMS

Joseph said God knows what dreams mean. Chat about dreams each person has had.

TRICKING PARENTS

Jacob tricked his dad, and his sons tricked him.
What happens when someone is tricked?

The brothers hated Joseph because their father loved him best. They never talked to Jacob about it. Talk about what upsets you in your family.

What is a famine?

FAMINES

Chat about countries where people are hungry now.
What can you do to help?

Travel Time

Let's go forward in the time tunnel to Matthew 1:21. *Wop, wop, wop!* An angel speaks to Joseph, telling him that Mary's Son was going to save people. God sent Jesus to deliver us.
Chat about how bad things happened to Jesus, too.

Matthew 1:21 She will give birth to a son, and you are to give him the name Jesus, because he will save his people from their sins.

Let's take another trip forward in the time tunnel to Romans 8:28. *Wop, wop, wop!* These words are a promise that God will use the bad times and events in our lives for good.
Chat about something bad God used for good in your family or your life.

Romans 8:28 And we know that in all things God works for the good of those who love him, who have been called according to his purpose.

Journal Time

Write or draw about ways to help feed hungry people.

Prayer Time

Dearest Father, thank You for using bad things for good. Help us trust that even in bad times You will bring good. Help our family love one another. Amen.

8 Moses and the Plagues

God's people, the children of Israel, stayed in Egypt four hundred years and became slaves. Pharaoh saw the Israelite nation had grown big so he tried to kill all baby boys. But Jochebed, Moses' mother, hid her baby in a basket on the river. Pharaoh's daughter found the basket and raised Moses as her own son.

Moses grew up. He saw an Egyptian beat an Israelite slave. He became angry and killed the Egyptian then ran away to the desert. He became a shepherd, married, and had two sons. One day Moses saw a burning bush on a mountaintop, but the bush didn't burn up.

Moses climbed the mountain to see it. God called to Moses and told him to take off his sandals because he stood on holy ground. God told Moses to go back to Egypt and free the Israelites. Moses said, "What do I say if the people ask what is God's name?" God replied, "I Am Who I Am." Moses asked God to send someone else. God grew angry but said Aaron, Moses' brother, would help.

When Moses went to Pharaoh, he asked him to free the people. Pharaoh said, "No." God sent a plague that turned all the water to blood and a plague of many frogs that jumped into every house. Still Pharaoh said, "No." God sent more plagues. He sent gnats to bite people, then a plague of many buzzing flies, and even a plague of disease that killed the Egyptian's animals. Still Pharaoh said, "No."

God sent a plague of boils, large painful sores, on people and a plague of hail that hit and killed every man and animal outside. The people had terrible problems with all these plagues, but Pharaoh still said, "No." He would not let God's people go! God sent a plague of locusts that ate all the plants, and then He sent a plague of darkness over the land. The Egyptians could not see for three

days and nights, although the Israelites had light.

Again Pharaoh said, "No!" God sent one more plague. He sent the angel of death to kill all the firstborn sons. He saved anyone who sprinkled the blood of a lamb on their door. He saved all the Israelites, and this is known as Passover because death passed over the Israelites. At long last Pharaoh said, "Go!"

Moses led the whole nation out of Egypt, thousands of people. Pharaoh changed his mind and sent his army after the people. But God sent a miracle. The Israelites were surrounded by mountains and the Red Sea. God lifted up the water to make a pathway. The Israelites crossed on dry land.

Hello.

My name is Moses, and I'm your new tour guide. I'm a member of Levi's family, one of Joseph's brothers. When God first asked me to tell others about Him, I felt scared. But I'm happy to tell you all about how God used me to help other people. Let's explore God's Word and find out what happened to Jacob's family in Egypt, many years after Jacob and Joseph died:

- *Listen to find out God's name.*
- *Find out how many plagues God sent.*
- *Discover what God did when His people were trapped between mountains, the sea, and an army.*

We'll chat about these ideas later.

Chat Time

Chat Word: *Freedom* means to not be under the control of someone, to not be their slave. Chat about having freedom to go to church.

PLAGUES

Plagues are a type of trouble that hurts many people.
Chat about the plagues God sent and why each bothered the people.
What plague sounds the worst to you and why?

MIRACLES

What is a miracle? When God's people were trapped, God opened the sea as a miracle.

What miracles has God done for your family?

NAMES

What did God say is His name?
Chat about how each person's name was chosen.
Does your last name have a meaning?

Travel Time

Let's go forward in the time tunnel to Galatians 5:1. *Wop, wop, wop!* It tells us that Christ set us free. He freed us not from leaders but from sin. **How can sin make someone a slave?**

Galatians 5:1 NASB It was for freedom that Christ set us free; therefore keep standing firm and do not be subject again to a yoke of slavery.

Chat about what Christ freed us from and what that means.

Journal Time

Write or draw about a miracle God did.

Prayer Time

Thank You, Father, for our freedom. Thank You also for the miracle of life You give us each day. Amen.

9 The Ten Commandments

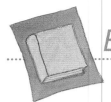
Hello.

I'm Moses, and I'm so happy to be with you again. Today I want to tell you about a mountain where God spoke after I led the people out of Egypt. God gave the people special rules. Let's explore what happened and find out about the rules:

- *Listen to find out how many times God wrote the rules.*
- *Find out how God wrote the rules.*
- *Discover what happened when Moses had too much work.*

We'll chat about these ideas later.

Three months after leaving Egypt, the Israelites came to Mount Sinai. Jethro, Moses' father-in-law, heard about this. He brought back Moses' wife and sons. They had stayed with Jethro while Moses went to Egypt. Jethro watched Moses work hard as a judge, settling problems. Jethro told Moses he needed men to help him. Moses chose leaders and solved only the hardest problems. This was so much better! Jethro went home.

God wanted to make a covenant with the people. He called Moses to the mountaintop. God said He would promise to care for the people and wanted them to promise to obey Him. He would give them special rules.

The people agreed. They washed their clothes to prepare for the promise. Moses drew a line around the bottom of the mountain and told the people to stay behind the line. Smoke puffed up from the mountain, and fire descended onto the mountain. The mountain shook, a horn blew, and lightning flashed. Moses climbed up. God told Moses to get his brother, Aaron.

Moses climbed down then climbed back up with Aaron. God told them many rules. Later, God told Moses to make two stone tablets and return. Moses took Joshua with him. They stayed with God forty days. God wrote the rules, called commandments, on the tablets with His finger.

Moses took so long that the people decided to make an idol. They gathered their gold jewelry and had Aaron melt it and shape it into a calf. They bowed down and worshiped the golden calf. When Moses returned and saw the people's sin, he became so angry that he threw the Ten Commandments to the ground. *Crash!* The tablets broke.

Moses ground the calf into powder, threw the powder into the river, and made the people drink the water. The water made people sick. Some of the people decided not to serve God. God had those people killed. The other people were sorry and agreed to obey God.

Moses climbed the mountain again. God wrote the Ten Commandments on new tablets. These are God's rules:

- I am God. Have no other gods.
- Do not worship idols.
- The Lord's name is holy. Use it only the right way.
- Keep the Lord's day holy.
- Honor your father and mother.
- Do not kill.
- Have sex only with your wife.
- Do not steal.
- Do not lie.
- Do not want your neighbor's wife or things.

When Moses returned, his face shone. This scared people so Moses wore a veil over his face. Moses led the people for many years.

Chat Word: *Commandment* means a rule given by someone in charge. Talk about God's commandments.

Chat Time

MORE LEADERS

Moses needed helpers. *Who helps lead your family?*
In our nation there are many leaders. Chat about those leaders and how they are chosen.

THE TEN COMMANDMENTS

Read the rules again and chat about each one and what it means.

Do not steal.

Do not lie.

Do not kill.

How did God write the rules?

How many times did He write the rules?

Do your parents ever have to tell you a rule more than one time?

The promise was another covenant.
Do you recall the covenant with Noah?

A SHINY FACE

Why do you think Moses had a shiny face?
Can people tell by looking at you if you know God?
How can people tell that you talk to God?

Travel Time

Let's travel forward in time. *Wop, wop, wop!* We are at Matthew 22:37-39. Wow! Jesus gives us a new commandment. This tells us the rules by telling us to love God and people.

Matthew 22:37-39 Jesus replied: " 'Love the Lord your God with all your heart and with all your soul and with all your mind.' This is the first and greatest commandment. And the second is like it: 'Love your neighbor as yourself.' "

Chat about these commandments.

Journal Time

Write or draw one way to love God.

Prayer Time

Thank You, God, for Your promises. Help me obey Your rules. Amen.

10 Manna and the Wanderings

Bible Time
Exodus 16-20; Numbers 13, 16

The Israelites felt so happy when they left Egypt! Miriam, the sister of Moses, led a huge parade, and everyone sang praises to God. Hurrah!

God wanted to bring the people to a new home, but it was a long trip. He cared for everyone while they traveled. Three days after leaving Egypt, the people looked around and saw desert everywhere. They were thirsty, but the river's water tasted bitter. They cried to Moses. God had Moses throw a tree into the waters that made the waters sweet.

The people looked around but saw no food. They grumbled, "Grrr, why did God bring us here? It would have been better to die in Egypt." So God sent bread from heaven. Every morning something called manna covered the ground. The manna looked like a seed, but it tasted like sweet crackers. God sent this miracle bread every day but the Sabbath. He sent twice as much the day before the Sabbath. God stayed with His people.

They made a worship tent with an altar and special box called the "Ark of My Word." Here the priests made sacrifices to God.

As they moved, God led them with a pillar of cloud all day and stayed with them every night in a pillar of

44

fire. They traveled far from the river and again cried to Moses for water. God had Moses strike a rock, and water poured out. God kept taking care of His people.

Enemies led by Amalek came to fight the Israelites. Joshua led the fight for Israel. Moses stood on a hill. When Moses lifted his arms to heaven, his people won, but when he felt tired and dropped his arms, the enemy won. Two men held Moses' arms up until the sun set and the Israelites won.

God showed the people the land where He wanted them to live. Moses sent twelve men to spy on the people living there. The men came back and showed Moses fruit from the land and said the land was good with plenty of room. Ten of the spies told everyone that the people there were too strong and big, like giants. Two of the men, Joshua and Caleb, disagreed. They said, "We can go there, for surely if God is pleased with us He will give us the land."

The people cried in fear and wanted to stone Joshua and Caleb. God became angry. As a punishment, He made the people wander in the desert for forty years. For those forty years God sent manna and gave them water. Their clothes lasted all those years. Even their shoes did not get holes or break for forty years. Moses saw the promised land but never entered it.

Good day.
It's me, Moses, again. After I helped free God's people and led them out of Egypt, God's people needed a place to live. God promised to bring them to a special land, a land flowing with milk and honey. Let's explore God's Word and find out what happened after the Israelites left Egypt:

- *Listen to the name of the food God sent.*
- *Find out how the people won a battle.*
- *Discover how God made bitter water taste sweet.*

We'll chat about these ideas later.

Chat Time

Chat Word: *Manna* means "What is it?" The people had never seen this type of food that God rained down from heaven. Chat about the miracle bread.

GOD CARES FOR HIS PEOPLE

God cared for the Israelites all those years.
What did He do?
How does God care for you?

TRUST

The people saw all God did yet felt afraid to go into the promised land.
Why?
Are you ever afraid because other people seem bigger than God?

History

PRAISE

The people felt so happy they sang and had a parade.
When have you felt happy as a family?
Do you ever sing praises to God or have a parade to thank Him?

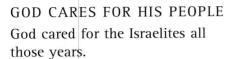

JESUS

46

Travel Time

Let's go forward in the time tunnel to John 6:48. *Wop, wop, wop!* God sent manna, a type of bread, to feed the people and keep them alive. God sent Jesus, called the Bread of Life, to give us eternal life.
Chat about how Jesus is the bread of life.

John 6:48
I am the
bread of life.

Journal Time

Write or draw about a time you sang praises.

Prayer Time

Dearest Father, thank You for caring for our family. Help us trust in You always. Amen.

11 Jericho and the Promised Land

Bible Time Joshua

Before Moses died he stood before the priest Eleazar and laid his hands on Joshua. The people understood God had chosen Joshua to lead them.

God spoke to Joshua and said that everywhere he stepped the land would belong to the Israelites. He told Joshua to think about His Word always. God promised to be with Joshua always.

Joshua sent two spies into the land and the city of Jericho. The spies stayed with Rahab, a bad woman. Men from Jericho heard of the spies and wanted to kill them, but Rahab hid the spies. She said the spies had left so the men went away. When she let the spies out from hiding, they promised to save her and her family if she would put a red ribbon in her window.

The spies returned to Joshua and said, "Surely God has given us this land." But, oh, no! Jericho and the promised land lay on the other side of the big Jordan River. The deep waters flowed over the sides of the riverbed.

Hooray! God had a plan. Joshua told the priests to carry the ark of the covenant and have the people follow. The ark was a gold-covered chest that held their most holy things: the Ten Commandments, a jar of manna, and Aaron's staff.

When the priests stepped into the Jordan, the river water stopped flowing. It stood back as though held by a dam. The people crossed on dry land. Then twelve men, one from each tribe, carried a large stone from the Jordan River to keep as a reminder of the miracle of crossing it. The priests crossed last, carrying the ark.

God gave Joshua a strange battle plan and sent the captain of the host of the Lord to help. For six days the people marched silently around Jericho. On day seven the people marched around the city seven times. After the march, Joshua yelled, "Shout! For the Lord has given you this city!" The people shouted! The priests blew trumpets! What roaring noise! *Kerplunk!* The walls of Jericho fell down flat, and the Israelites won! They saved Rahab, who chose to live with

them and follow God's laws.

God helped them win more battles, one with hail hitting the enemies and one with God making the sun and moon stand still for a day. Joshua divided the land, giving each tribe room to live.

Joshua read the words of the law and told the people to choose whom they would serve, idols or God. He said, "As for me and my family, we will serve the Lord." The people chose to serve the Lord. Joshua died at 110 years old.

Hi there!

My name is Joshua, and I'm your tour guide. Remember when Moses sent twelve spies into Canaan? I'm one of those twelve. My friend Caleb and I said, "Let's go and take the land," but the people were too afraid. God chose me to be the leader when Moses died.

- *Find out about God's unusual battle plan.*
- *Discover what woman in Jericho helped us.*

Chat Time

Chat Word: Joshua saw a man holding a sword who spoke and said he was the *captain of God's army*. People believe this was Jesus.
Chat about how we know the Lord is with us.

THE ARK OF THE COVENANT

The ark and rocks reminded people of God's presence and miracles.

What reminds you of God's presence?

STRANGE BATTLES

How funny did it seem to have walls of a city fall down from shouting?

Can you think of a time when God gave you a strange answer to help you with a problem?

CHOOSING TO SERVE GOD

Who does your family serve, God or an idol?

An idol is a false god. Money or a toy can be an idol if we worship it. Joshua said his family, and everyone in his house, would serve God.

What does it mean to serve God?

Travel Time

Let's go forward in the time tunnel to Ephesians 6:12. *Wop, wop, wop!* Wow! God's Word tells us that we have spiritual battles and special weapons. If we read more we discover spiritual weapons of prayer, truth, and the gospel.
Talk about shields of faith and other spiritual weapons.

Ephesians 6:12 For our struggle is not against flesh and blood, but against the rulers, against the authorities, against the powers of this dark world and against the spiritual forces of evil in the heavenly realms.

Journal Time

Write or draw about a way to serve God.

Prayer Time

Dear Lord, be with us in all our battles and struggles. Thanks for showing us You control the weather and can do anything to help Your people! Help us serve You always. Amen.

12 The Judges— Deborah and Gideon

After Joshua died, the older men who served with Joshua led the people. After these leaders died, the people forgot God, worshiped idols, and chose to be bad. God became angry and let their enemies fight and win.

Each time the people sinned and God let enemies win, they cried to God for help. God sent people called judges to lead the Israelites. God used judges to turn the people's hearts back to God. Once a judge died, the people sinned again until God chose a new judge. In all, God sent twelve judges. Two of these, Deborah and Gideon, were very special.

Deborah sat under a palm tree and settled people's problems. At this time a man named Sisera led the enemies of Israel and was very mean to God's people. Deborah called Barak and told him to lead an army against Sisera. Barak

---

Hi!
It's me, Joshua. I want to tell you what happened to God's people after I died. The people forgot God and things got bad. But then God gave the people new leaders, called judges.

- *Find out what judge used a fleece and what that means.*
- *Discover how God used a woman judge.*

52

agreed to go if Deborah went. She went, and the Israelites won. Deborah and Barak sang a great song of praise to God.

Later, when Midianites took control of the Israelites, God called Gideon to judge and save the people. Gideon asked, "How can I help, a weak man from a weak family?" The Lord answered, "I and My strength will be with you." God told Gideon to destroy the altar to Baal and build one to Him. Gideon did this at night but still wondered if God really wanted to use him. He asked for a sign.

Gideon laid a fleece (that's an animal skin) on the ground. He asked God to keep the ground dry and let the fleece be wet with dew. God did, but Gideon asked for another sign. This time he asked God to wet the ground and keep the fleece dry. God did that, too, then Gideon believed and left to fight for God.

God had an unusual battle plan. Gideon gathered 32,000 men to fight, but God chose only three hundred of the men to fight the large enemy army. He chose only the men who stood at the river and drank with one hand while holding a weapon in the other hand. He didn't have the men use weapons but instead had them carry trumpets and jugs with fiery torches inside. Gideon divided the men into three groups. They marched to the enemies' camp. *Crash*, they smashed the jugs, blew the trumpets, and carried the torches. This surprise attack confused the enemy. Gideon and his men won the battle. The people asked Gideon and his grandson to rule them. Gideon said no, that God would rule the people. As soon as Gideon died, the people forgot God again.

God let enemies win again and chose more judges to rule.

Chat Time

Chat Word: *Leader.* A leader is a guide, a person who tells or shows others what to do. Chat about how parents are the leaders in the home.

LEADERS

Gideon and Deborah worked and celebrated with their people.
What do your parents do to lead you?

FOLLOWERS

People who listen to a leader and obey are followers. ***Who do you follow?***
When a leader died, the people forgot God. What do you do when a leader is not watching you?
How can you be a good follower of God?

HISTORY

Who can help you become a good leader?

BIBLE

REMEMBERING GOD

The people kept forgetting God.
What helps you remember God?

Travel Time

Let's go forward in the time tunnel to Mark 8:34. *Wop, wop, wop!* This brings us to Jesus. He said we must deny, or forget, ourselves and follow Him.
What does it mean to forget ourselves?

Mark 8:34 Then he called the crowd to him along with his disciples and said: "If anyone would come after me, he must deny himself and take up his cross and follow me."

Journal Time

Write or draw something God did for you. It can remind you of God.

Pray

Read the BIBLE

God's creativity

Listen to God

Prayer Time

God, our Father, help us to keep our eyes and hearts on You. You were patient when Gideon wasn't sure You spoke to him. Help us trust when You speak to us. Help us remember You and obey You. Amen.

13 Samuel, a Prophet and Priest Who Listened to God

Bible Time 1 Samuel

Hannah and Elkanah took their young son Samuel, whom they loved, to the temple. They told Eli the priest that Samuel was an answer to prayer and that they had promised to give their son to serve the Lord all his life. They left Samuel at the temple. Each year when Samuel's family traveled to the temple to worship, Hannah gave her son a robe she made for him.

One night, after Samuel went to sleep, he woke because he heard someone call, "Samuel." He ran to Eli, but Eli had not called him. After this happened three times, Eli told the boy that God was calling him. The next time, Samuel answered, "Speak, Thy servant is listening." God spoke to Samuel that night and for many years. Samuel listened and obeyed God. Samuel served as a prophet, priest, and judge for a long time.

Eli's sons made a bad choice. They took the holy ark of the covenant to the army's camp to help win a battle. The enemy, the Philistines, won the battle and took the Ark away. Eli's sons died, and when Eli heard what happened, he fell down and died. The Philistines put the ark in a house of an idol god. The Philistines became sick. *Crash*, their idol statue broke! They had trouble from the time they took the ark until they gave it back to God's people.

After the enemy returned the ark, Samuel gathered the people and led them in turning their hearts back to God. God helped them. He sent thunder to confuse the enemy, and the Israelites won. God gave the people peace.

When Samuel grew old the people asked for a king. Samuel asked God about it, and God told him to tell the people how a king would change their lives. A king would make everyone serve him instead of God. The people still cried for a king. God chose Saul. Samuel anointed Saul. The people liked Saul because he looked handsome.

King Saul ruled for forty-two years. He won battles and led well but started making bad choices. He turned away from God. God felt bad that He had made Saul king and sent Samuel to choose another man to be king.

Samuel traveled to Bethlehem to Jesse's home. He looked at each son of Jesse but did not find the right person. He asked Jesse if he had another son. Jesse said he had a little son, David, who took care of the sheep. Samuel sent for David, saying God sees the heart and not only outward looks. David loved God with his whole heart. Hooray! God chose David. Samuel anointed David but died before David really became king.

Hello.

My name is Hannah and I'm your tour guide. I cried and prayed to God for a child. I promised if God gave me a son I would give the child to Him. God answered my prayer. I gave birth to Samuel the next year.

- *Find out who kept calling Samuel during the night.*
- *Discover why Samuel anointed a new king.*

57

Chat Time

Chat Word: A *priest* in the Old Testament was from the tribe of Levi. He was a spiritual leader. Only the *priest* could offer a sacrifice.
Chat about the leaders in your church.

LISTENING

Listen means to open your ears and really hear the words people say. When someone else talks, stop and think about the words.
Do you listen to your church leaders? To your parents?
Chat about a time when someone didn't listen to you.

INSIDE A HEART

What does God see in your heart?

When you have anger or bad things in your heart, what can you do?

PRAYER

Hannah asked for a baby.
Why do you think God gave Hannah a baby?
Did your parents ask God for you or were you a surprise gift?

PUTTING GOD FIRST

Eli's sons moved the ark without asking God.
What happened because they forgot to ask God?
Do you remember to ask God about your ideas before doing things?

Travel Time

Let's go forward in the time tunnel to Hebrews 4:14. *Wop, wop, wop!* Wow! We find out that Jesus is our high priest. **What does Jesus do as a priest?**

Hebrews 4:14 Therefore, since we have a great high priest who has gone through the heavens, Jesus the Son of God, let us hold firmly to the faith we profess.

Journal Time

Write or draw yourself listening to God's Word.

Prayer Time

Dear Father, help us listen to You and one another. Thank You for answering prayers and sending good spiritual leaders. Help us remember and obey the words we hear. Amen.

14 Saul, a Leader Who Turned from God

Saul never expected to be king. While he was searching for his father's donkeys, the prophet Samuel found him and told him that God and the people wanted him for king. Saul said, "But am I not a Benjamite, from the smallest tribe of Israel?"

Samuel anointed Saul and gave him signs to show God wanted him for king. He said Saul would pass three men, one carrying three young goats, one carrying three loaves of bread, and one carrying a jug of wine. Samuel said the men would give Saul two loaves of bread. Samuel also told Saul that when he met prophets parading, Saul would receive power from God and would prophesy. It all happened! Samuel warned Saul to wait for him for seven days when he later went to Gilgal.

The Ammonites fought the Israelites who lived in Jabesh-Gilead. The people asked for a treaty. The Ammonite king said, "All right, but I will make everyone blind in one eye to shame your people."

Saul heard about the problem and led the people in a battle against the enemy. Saul won. The people celebrated and rejoiced that God chose Saul as king. Tall Saul looked so good!

Saul chose men to fight against the Philistines. He chose his son Jonathan to be one of the leaders. The army went and camped at Gilgal. They waited six days but then the men got tired of waiting. Saul felt afraid that his men would leave. Saul was not a priest. *Oops!* On the seventh day he made a sacrifice to God. Samuel came after the sacrifice and said, "You acted foolishly!" Because Saul did not wait for a priest to make the offering, his kingdom would not last. Saul felt sorry.

When Saul fought the enemy, he won. He fought enemies to the east, west, north, and south. He won every time! Saul's army fought the Philistines all the days of Saul.

But Saul did not always obey God. His men took things that belonged to their enemies. Saul went to see someone who tried to speak to the dead. Saul lied when Samuel spoke to him about his sins then felt sorry again. God told Saul to destroy his enemy, every last person. Oh, no! Saul disobeyed again! He saved the enemy's king, Agag. God felt sorry that He had made Saul king. God chose David, a man who loved God, to be the next king.

At first Saul liked David. David helped King Saul defeat a giant named Goliath and to win battles against the Philistines. When Saul found out that God wanted David to be the new king, he became very jealous. He tried to kill David and chased him out of Israel.

Chat Time

Chat Word: A *king* is a leader with total control over his people and land. Chat about the leaders in your country. Who are they, and do they make all the decisions?

WAITING

Tick, tock! Saul and the men grew tired of waiting. They were impatient.
Have you ever been tired of waiting for a prayer answer?
What can help you wait, even for a long time?

OBEDIENCE

Homework

Saul sometimes disobeyed.
Have you ever disobeyed God or someone?
When Samuel talked to Saul about being disobedient, Saul lied.
Why was that even worse?

LEADERS

Samuel was a priest, a spiritual leader. Saul was an earthly leader.
Chat about the two leaders. Who was good?
What signs did God show Saul?
How does it help a leader to listen and obey God?

Travel Time

Let's go forward in the time tunnel. *Wop, wop, wop!* to 1 Timothy 1:17. This tells us that God is the one real king who will be king forever!
Chat about how God is a good king.

1 Timothy 1:17 Now to the King eternal, immortal, invisible, the only God, be honor and glory for ever and ever. Amen.

Journal Time

Write or draw about a time you waited for God to answer.

Prayer Time

Thank You, God, for being a good king, for caring for Your people. Help us wait for Your answers. Amen.

63

15 David, a Man with a Heart for God

Bible Time 1 Samuel 16–18; 2 Samuel

Samuel filled his horn with oil, went to Bethlehem, and bought a cow to sacrifice. He was really looking for the new king. Samuel found and anointed David, Jesse's youngest boy.

King Saul didn't know about Samuel anointing David. Saul wanted someone to play the harp for him and heard that David played well and sent for him. David spent his time playing the harp, singing songs about God, called psalms, and tending his father's sheep. David's brothers became soldiers.

One day, Jesse sent David to take food to his brothers. When David found his brothers he learned about a big problem. Goliath, a nine-foot-tall giant, scared all the soldiers. Goliath told the Israelites to send out one man to fight him. He said the loser's people would be the slaves of the winner's people. The Israelites ran and hid when they saw Goliath. David told King Saul that he would fight Goliath.

Saul said, "You are only a boy."

David argued, "When a lion or bear scared the sheep, I killed it. God, who saved me from the paws of the lion and the bear, will save me from this Philistine giant."

David grabbed five stones out of a nearby brook, took his sling, then marched up to Goliath. David shouted, "I come to you in the name of God!" He swung his sling, *whirl* went the stone, and up, up, up, in the air it flew. The stone hit Goliath on his forehead. Crash! Goliath fell and died.

Saul gave David treasures and his daughter for a wife. David became great friends with Saul's son Jonathan. David led Saul's army to victory. Hooray! People praised David. Saul became jealous and tried to kill David. Jonathan helped David escape.

After Saul and his sons died, David became king. He beat the Philistines. The people rejoiced and built a palace in Jerusalem. Other

enemies tried to beat the Israelites. David asked God for help.

God sent David behind the enemies to listen for marching sounds in the tree tops. It meant God was there, fighting, too. David's army won.

David moved the ark of God to Jerusalem. He sent his army to fight another enemy, but he stayed home. One day David saw a beautiful woman on the palace roof. David had two wives, but he wanted this woman, Bathsheba, too. Her husband was a soldier. David sinned, and Bathsheba had David's baby. David had her husband killed, then married her.

God sent a prophet to talk to David about his sins. David felt very sorry. God forgave David but let that baby die. Later Bathsheba had another baby named Solomon. God loved Solomon. David ruled as king for forty years.

Hello.

I'm Ruth, your new tour guide. I was a poor widow after my husband died. Later I met Boaz, a wheat farmer, worked in his fields, and then married him. It's time to learn about David, my great-grandson:

- *Find out what instrument David played.*
- *Discover what helped give David courage to fight a giant.*

Chat Time

Chat Word: *Anoint* means to pour costly oil, mixed with spices, on someone. Priests anointed a king to show God had chosen him as ruler. The word *Christ* means "anointed one."
Chat about why Jesus is called the anointed one.

FIGHTING GIANTS

Why wasn't David afraid to fight the giant?

Does it help to remember how God has helped you in the past?

A HEART FOR GOD

God said David was a man after God's own heart.
Was David always perfect? What do you think it means to have a heart after God's own heart?

SINS AND FORGIVENESS

When the prophet spoke to David about his sins, David did not lie. David said he was sorry and prayed.
What do you do after you do something wrong?

Travel Time

Let's go forward in the time tunnel to 1 Timothy 6:15. *Wop, wop, wop!* to the days after Jesus rose. Here the apostle Paul tells us Jesus is our king. **Chat about how Jesus is king, or ruler, of all.**

1 Timothy 6:15 NASB Which He [Jesus Christ] will bring about at the proper time—He who is the blessed and only Sovereign, the King of kings and Lord of lords.

Journal Time

Draw a crown for Jesus.

Prayer Time

Lord, Jesus, King of kings, how wonderful that You forgive people when they are sorry for doing bad things. Help us to have hearts full of love for You. Amen.

16 Psalms

God's people spoke with God. They worshiped Him in songs, they praised Him and thanked Him for His mighty deeds. They cried to Him in troubled times and asked for forgiveness when they sinned.

Moses prayed (Psalm 90) a psalm of prayer with the words "Lord, You have been our dwelling place throughout all generations. Before the mountains were born or you brought forth the earth and the world, from everlasting to everlasting you are God." He ended the psalm with, "May the favor of the Lord our God rest upon us; establish the work of our hands."

King David watched his father's sheep as a young boy and wrote many psalms. One (Psalm 23) began with, "The LORD is my shepherd, I shall not be in want." He told how God gives comfort: "I will fear no evil for you are with me." He ended with, "Surely goodness and love will follow me all the days of my life, and I will dwell in the house of the LORD forever."

When David fought enemies, he wrote psalms asking for help. David sang (Psalm 25), "To you, O LORD, I lift up my soul; in you I trust, O my God. Do not let me be put to shame, nor let my enemies triumph over me."

The Israelites thanked God (Psalm 30) when they dedicated the temple, Gods' house, singing, "O LORD my God, I will give you thanks forever."

When he sinned, David asked for God's forgiveness (Psalm 51). He cried, "Have mercy on me, O God...blot out all my iniquity," and, "Create in me a pure heart."

The choir leaders were sons of Korah who led the people in singing psalms that they wrote to help people remember God's miracles. In one song they recalled the past (Psalm 44), "Our fathers have told us what you did in their days. . . . With your hand you drove out the nations."

Good day!
It's me, Ruth. Today you will learn about special songs of praise, called psalms. My great-grandson David wrote many of the psalms.

- *Find out some of the types of psalms.*
- *Discover how a psalm tells what happened when you grew inside your mom.*

A prophet, Asaph, taught the people with psalms about messages from God. In one (Psalm 81 by Asaph) God said, "I am the LORD your God, who brought you up out of Egypt. Open wide your mouth and I will fill it."

Psalms also prophesied of the coming Messiah. The words told people what would happen (Psalm 22), "They have pierced my hands and my feet." "They divide my garments among them and cast lots for my clothing," and (Psalm 69), "They. . .gave me vinegar for my thirst."

People sang psalms to celebrate God's love and care. The words showed God's loving power (Psalm 139), "O LORD, you have searched me and you know me," "For you created my inmost being; you knit me together in my mother's womb."

Chat Time

Chat Word: A *psalm* is a song about God.
Can you make up your own psalm about God?

PRAISING GOD

Why do you think it helps us to praise Him? When you sing and praise God, what do you think about?

PRAISING GOD

Does it help you forget your problems and remember to trust God?

PSALMS ABOUT GOD'S LOVE

Think of a song you like that tells about God loving you.
Why do you like it?

Talk about how God loved you even when you were inside your mom.

SAD PSALMS

Psalms are another way to pray. Some psalms were cries for help.
Do you ever feel like crying to God for help?
Chat about a time you cried, and God helped.

Travel Time

Let's travel forward to Revelation 4:10. *Wop, wop, wop!*
Listen to the words. Everyone in heaven is singing to God.
Chat about singing in heaven.

Revelation 4:10 The twenty-four elders fall down before
him who sits on the throne, and worship him who lives
forever and ever. They lay their crowns before the
throne. . . .

Journal Time

Write or draw about your favorite song.

Prayer Time

Lord, we thank You and praise You. Thank You for giving us voices to sing.
Amen.

17 Wise King Solomon

David had many sons. He chose his son Solomon to be the next king. He sent Solomon to ride his mule with the prophet Nathan shouting, "Long live King Solomon!" Zadok, the priest, poured oil on Solomon's head.

David said, "Be strong and follow God. Serve Him with your whole heart and willing mind." David died at age seventy. Long before he died, David said God needed a temple.

God would not let David build the temple because he fought battles. God chose Solomon, a peaceful king, to build the temple. God even chose Solomon's name, which means "peaceful." David collected the money needed for the temple and shared with Solomon the plans for the temple.

When he became king, Solomon gave offerings to God. In a dream, God said, "Ask for whatever you wish."

"I want an understanding heart," Solomon said. This pleased God. He made Solomon the wisest man who ever lived.

People and leaders came from everywhere to learn from Solomon. He amazed the Queen of Sheba with his wisdom, and she gave him gifts, saying, "You are even wiser than I had heard."

Solomon made wise choices for his people. Two women each had a baby, but one baby died. One woman said the other tricked her and switched the dead baby for her live baby during the night.

Hello again.

It's me, Ruth, and I'm here to tell you about my great-great-grandson, Solomon, son of King David, and Solomon's great wisdom.

- *Find out how Solomon became wise.*
- *Discover what Solomon built.*

They asked Solomon to pick the right mother. What a hard choice! Solomon took a sword and said he would cut the baby in half, one half for each. One woman cried, "No! let the other woman keep the baby." Solomon knew the one who wanted to save the baby was the real mother and gave her the baby.

In his fourth year as king, Solomon started building the temple, using the best materials. It took seven years to finish. The priests carried the ark of God into the new temple and made sacrifices. Solomon prayed, "God, be with us." God sent fire from heaven that swallowed the sacrifices.

Soon after, God spoke to Solomon, "I heard your prayer. I have blessed the temple." God told Solomon to follow His laws and be sure the people followed them, too. If they followed God, He would bless them. If they turned away, He would send trouble.

Solomon's people lived in peace. Solomon wrote many wise sayings, called proverbs. Solomon also made some bad choices. As a young man he married a woman not for love but to make friends with her country. He married many women and let them keep idols. As he grew old, his wives turned his heart away from God. This angered God, who said He would take most of the kingdom away from Solomon's son.

Chat Time

Chat Word: *Wisdom* means to think clearly and make good choices.
Chat about wise and foolish choices.

WISDOM
How did Solomon get wisdom?

WISDOM

Can you ask God for wisdom?
Look up James 1:5 to find out.

FOLLOWING GOD
What did God say would happen if Solomon did not follow God?

FOLLOWING GOD
What happens when you forget to obey God?

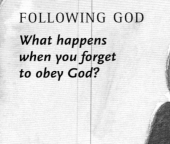

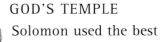

GOD'S TEMPLE
Solomon used the best wood and things to build a temple for God.

When we give something to God, should we give our best?

How can you help care for your church building?

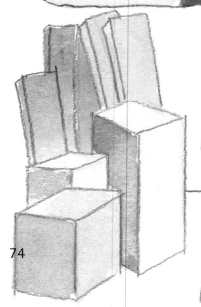

Travel Time

Let's go forward in the time tunnel to John 14:26. *Wop, wop, wop!* It's Jesus talking. He says that the Holy Spirit will teach us.
Chat about how the Holy Spirit of God helps us be wise.

John 14:26: But the Counselor, the Holy Spirit, whom the Father will send in my name, will teach you all things and will remind you of everything I have said to you.

Journal Time

Draw or write about your church building.

JESUS

PEACE

BIBLE

Prayer Time

Father, thank You for giving us wise words in the Bible. Help us learn what the words mean and help us make wise choices. Amen.

18 More Kings

Bible Time 1 Kings 12-2 Kings

Rehoboam, son of Solomon, became king. Before Solomon died, the prophet Ahijah said Jeroboam would lead most of the Israelites. Jeroboam and many people went to King Rehoboam. They asked, "Will you be mean like King Solomon?"

Rehoboam, who listened to bad advice, said, "Yes! Yes! I will be meaner than my father." This upset many people. They chose to follow Jeroboam instead. This split Israel into two nations.

People named King Rehoboam's nation Judah, as the kings were from the tribe of Judah. Their land had God's temple in Jerusalem.

People called King Jeroboam's nation of ten tribes Israel. They lived in the north with no temple. Jeroboam worried that the people would leave to worship God in the temple. He sinned by making gold calves for people to worship and making people priests who were not Levites. God did not let his family live.

After Jeroboam, many more kings ruled Israel in the north. Oh, no! These kings disobeyed God, too. Ahab, the eighth king of Israel, worshiped Baal, a false god, and did great evil in God's eyes.

Jehu, anointed king by Elisha, tried to get rid of all who worshiped Baal, but he served God half-heartedly. He worshiped the golden calf. After him, more bad kings led the people to disobey God. God allowed their enemy, the Assyrians, to capture the people and take them far away from their land.

In Judah, the southern kingdom, King Rehoboam and his people forgot God's laws, so God let the Egyptians take away their treasures. After Rehoboam, more kings ruled Judah. Many disobeyed God, but a few loved and served Him. Hooray! Asa, a good king, tore down many idols and understood that when you are with God, He is with you. But oh, no! Asa forgot to trust God as he grew old and died from a sickness that he never asked God to heal.

After Asa, King Jehoshaphat also loved God. Yea! Mostly, he followed God and made good choices. He made sure the people learned about God. Oh, no! After King Jehoshaphat, other kings led people in sinning again.

Then, Hezekiah, the thirteenth king, loved God and always prayed to Him. He destroyed all idols in Judah and turned the people's hearts back to God. He foolishly showed his enemies the temple treasures that they later took.

Josiah became the sixteenth king, at age eight. Josiah loved God with his whole heart. When he heard God's laws read, he understood the sin of his people. Because this upset him, Josiah tore his clothes and wept. Because of Josiah's love, God kept the people safe. Later kings sinned, so God let the Babylonians take the people away as slaves.

Hello.
I'm Elijah, a prophet sent by God to tell the kings to obey God's laws. I want you to learn about the kings after Solomon.

- *Find out about the good kings.*
- *Discover why the kingdom became two kingdoms.*

Chat Time

Chat Word: A *kingdom* is the country where a king lives and rules. Jesus called heaven a kingdom. Chat about what heaven might be like.

FOLLOWING LEADERS

With a good king, people were good.
With a bad king, people were bad.
If someone you like is bad, how can you keep from following him?

THE TROUBLE WITH MEANNESS
What happened because a king chose to be mean?

Why do we need Jesus as our king?

BEING SORRY

Why did Josiah cry?
Have you ever been really sorry for something?
What did God do because of Josiah?

Does it hurt when someone is mean?

What can you do when someone is mean?

sweets

Travel Time

Let's go forward a little bit in the time tunnel to Daniel 2:44. *Wop, wop, wop!* Here another prophet tells us about the future, about God's kingdom that is yet to come.

Chat about how God's kingdom will last forever.

Daniel 2:44 In the time of those kings, the God of heaven will set up a kingdom that will never be destroyed, nor will it be left to another people.

Journal Time

Draw or write about how you will feel in God's kingdom.

Prayer Time

Dear Father, give us good leaders on earth. Thank You, Jesus, for being such a good leader and king. Help us be like You. Amen.

79

19 Elijah the Prophet

Bible Time 1 Kings 17–21; 2 Kings 2

When kings ruled Israel, God called a hairy man, named Elijah, to be a prophet.

Elijah told King Ahab that no rain would fall for three years. Ahab worshiped idols, especially Baal, and God stopped the rain as a warning. Not one drop of water fell from the sky!

Crops couldn't grow, rivers dried up, and people had little food. God sent Elijah to a poor widow of Zarephath. He found her picking up sticks.

He asked for water and bread.

She said, "My son and I are hungry. I have only a little flour and oil. With these sticks I will make a fire and cook a meal so we may eat before we die."

Elijah said, "Don't be afraid. Cook a cake for me and for you and your son. God says your jar of flour and jug of oil will not be empty until rain comes again." It all came true!

Some time later her son became ill and stopped breathing. Elijah prayed, and God restored the boy's life.

The king and people worshiped Baal, so Elijah dared them to a contest. He would put a bull on an altar for God, and they would put a bull out for Baal. No one could light a fire except by prayer. Baal's 850 leaders cried for hours, but no fire came. People poured twelve buckets of water on Elijah's wood and bull. Elijah prayed, "God, send fire to show Your power."

Fire fell from heaven and burned the bull, wood, stone altar, and even the dirt and water! The people believed in God when they saw that!

Three years had passed so Elijah said rain would come.

His servant looked seven times and finally saw a tiny cloud at sea. The cloud brought a great rain. Elijah heard the king's wife, Jezebel, wanted to kill him. He ran away then until God spoke. God told him He would pass by. *Swish*! Strong winds blew. *Boom*, an earthquake came! *Crackle*, a fire passed. God wasn't in those. Then in a soft, gentle blowing, Elijah heard God.

"Go back," God said. "Make Elisha the next prophet." He found Elisha plowing a field. Elisha went with Elijah. One day, Elijah asked Elisha, "Do you know God is taking me today?" Elisha knew. He stayed with Elijah and asked for two times as much of Elijah's spirit. This meant he wanted to take Elijah's place as prophet. Elijah said this would happen if Elisha saw how God took him.

Elisha looked and saw Elijah go up to heaven in a whirlwind. Wind swirled and swished around Elijah. Elisha saw Elijah no more. God used Elisha to be His next prophet and to do miracles.

Hello.
It's me, Elijah, the prophet. Today you'll learn about amazing things God did because I obeyed Him.

- *Find out about the fire God sent from heaven.*
- *Discover how I went to heaven.*

81

Chat Time

Chat Word: A *prophet* is a special messenger chosen by God to tell people about God and sometimes to tell them about the future.

NO FOOD
Chat about how God saved the widow and her son.
Have you ever been hungry?

Do you thank God for giving you food?

LISTENING TO GOD

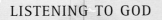

Chat about how God heard Elijah's prayer and sent fire.

When God passed by, what did Elijah hear?

THE CONTEST
Elijah stood alone against 850 people who believed in Baal.
Chat about why Elijah wanted God to send the fire for the sacrifice.

Is it hard to stand for God alone?

Travel Time

Let's go forward in the time tunnel to the New Testament days, to Matthew 17:3. *Wop, wop, wop!* Here the apostles see Jesus talking with Elijah. **Chat about how Elijah could be there hundreds of years after he went to heaven.**

Matthew 17:3 Just then there appeared before them [Peter, James, John] Moses and Elijah, talking with Jesus.

Journal Time

Draw or write about telling others about Jesus.

Prayer Time

Father, we thank You for always standing with us. Help us to have the courage to speak out about You. We are happy to know that we, too, will go to heaven one day. Help us to hear Your words. Amen.

20 Jonah and Nineveh

Bible Time Jonah

Crash! A great storm rocked the ship and scared the sailors. They prayed to idol gods and asked each other what caused the storm. The captain saw Jonah sleeping. He woke him up.

Jonah was a prophet, not a sailor. Jonah obeyed God when he told King Jeroboam II his people would win back the land of Israel in a battle. But when God asked Jonah to preach to wicked people in Nineveh, Jonah ran away. He bought a ticket and sailed on the ship going away from Nineveh!

The sailors cast lots (that's like drawing straws) to find who caused trouble. The lot fell on Jonah. The men cried, "Who are you, and what have you done?"

Jonah said, "I'm running from God."

Crash! Swish! Waves came higher, almost breaking the ship to pieces! The men cried, "How can we stop this terrible storm?"

"Throw me into the sea." said Jonah.

The men worked harder to row to shore. They couldn't do it. They prayed to God, "Don't let us die because Jonah sinned. Don't blame us if he dies." They picked up Jonah. *Splash!* They threw him into the sea. Hush. The storm stopped. The sailors believed in God.

"Gulp!" A great fish swallowed Jonah. Jonah stayed there for three days and nights. At last he prayed. He thanked God for saving him from drowning. He promised to obey God. SSSSPIT! The fish spit Jonah up on dry land.

Jonah went to Nineveh and walked through the city for three days, shouting. He said God would destroy Nineveh in forty days.

The king of Nineveh and his people listened. They believed Jonah and knew they were wicked. The king dressed in clothes made of old sacks to show he felt sorry. He sat in dirt and told his people not to eat or drink anything. He asked them to dress in sacks, too, and to pray, hoping God would change His mind.

God had mercy. He let the people live.

This upset Jonah. He said, "God, I know You are loving and could stop from destroying Nineveh. I'd rather die since nothing I shouted will happen."

God asked, "Do you have any right to be angry?"

Jonah left the city, made a little shelter, and sat in it. God made a vine grow that shaded Jonah. Jonah liked the vine. Munch! Munch! The next day God sent a worm that ate the vine. The sun rose. The hot sun made Jonah weak. He wanted to die.

God asked, "Do you have the right to be angry that I let the vine die?"

Jonah answered, "Yes."

God said, "You care about the vine although I made it. I care about the people."

Chat Time

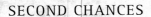

Chat Word: *Repent* means to be sorry for what you have done and to want to change to be better.

Chat about ways you have changed because you were sorry about a sin.

SECOND CHANCES

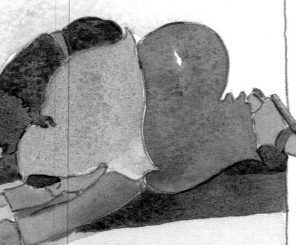

God gave the people time to repent and change.

Do you always give people another chance when they hurt you?

Is it hard to forgive someone bad even though God forgives them?

SITTING IN DIRT

The king and people sat in dirt to show they were sorry.

How do you show someone you are sorry?

What helps you do God's work?

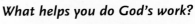

RUNNING FROM GOD

Do you always want to do what God wants you to do?

Travel Time

Let's go forward in the time tunnel to Matthew 12:40. *Wop, wop, wop!* Jesus tells people that Jonah was a sign about how Jesus would be dead for three days.
Chat about Jonah being inside the fish for three days.

Matthew 12:40 For as Jonah was three days and three nights in the belly of a huge fish, so the Son of Man will be three days and three nights in the heart of the earth.

Journal Time

Draw or write about something God wants you to do that is hard for you.

Prayer Time

Thank You, Jesus, for dying for us. It must have been hard to die and be buried. Thank You for forgiving us every time we make the wrong choice. Help us forgive other people who are bad and help us pray for them and tell them about You. Amen.

21 Isaiah and His Prophecies

Bible Time 2 Kings 19-20; Isaiah

The prophet Isaiah heard God speak and saw pictures in his mind, called visions. God told Isaiah about the future through the visions.

Isaiah saw God sitting on a throne in heaven. Winged angels, called seraphs, worshiped God.

"Woe!" Isaiah cried. "My lips are dirty with sin, and I am in trouble now!"

An angel flew and touched Isaiah's lips with a burning coal from God's altar. It took away Isaiah's sin.

God asked, "Who will be our messenger?"

"Here I am. Send me!" called Isaiah.

God said, "Go and tell the people."

Isaiah told the people many things. He prophesied during the lives of four kings of Israel. He spoke about wars. One king, Hezekiah, prayed for help when the Assyrian army marched to destroy Jerusalem, the holy city.

Isaiah told the king, "The Lord says, 'I will defend my city.'"

That night God sent angels out who destroyed the enemy.

Later, King Hezekiah became so sick he thought he would die. Isaiah said God would heal him. As a sign, the sun's shadow went back ten steps.

Isaiah told of pictures about Israel.

"I saw a grape vineyard on a hill. I took out stones and planted it. I cut a tub from rock for making wine. But only bad grapes grew! Now I will cut down the vineyard and let weeds grow."

God says, "Israel is like the vineyard. I care for them but they do bad things. I will teach them by letting enemies take them away."

Isaiah saw how the Messiah would come. "A virgin will have a baby named Immanuel. He will be a great light, the Prince of Peace, and sit on David's throne."

Isaiah also saw the Messiah's death.

"I see them strike his back, spit on his face, and pierce his side. He dies for our sins. He is killed like a silent lamb."

Isaiah saw God judge enemies who were mean to Israel.

"Woe to Babylon! Only wild goats and owls will live there. And jackals and hyenas will howl there."

"Woe to Tyre. You have no more houses or harbors."

"Woe to Egypt. Your people will become slaves, barefoot and naked."

"Woe to the Philistines, Moabites, Assyrians, Cushites, and more. I will destroy all Israel's enemies."

How sad for those who hurt Israel! Isaiah saw good for people who love God. Hooray! He saw God give a big party on top of Mount Zion with the best food and drinks. No one would die anymore.

In his last vision Isaiah saw God create a new heaven and new earth.

God called, "Rejoice! The wolf will live with the lamb, and the lion will eat straw like the oxen."

Hello.
I'm Daniel, and I'm your new tour guide. You'll hear about my adventures with lions and writing on the wall later. It's time now to find out about Isaiah, a prophet who told the Israelites much about the coming of the Messiah.

- *Find out about Isaiah's first job, in a palace.*

- *Discover one prophecy Isaiah told about Jesus, the Messiah.*

Chat Time

Chat Word: A *vision* is a picture sent from God that you see in your mind.
Chat about the difference between a dream and a vision.

VISIONS

Isaiah saw lions eating straw and other strange visions.
Why do you think God told Isaiah things in visions?
How does God tell us things?

SPEAKING OUT FOR GOD

Isaiah told everyone what God said, even if it made them angry.
Are you willing to tell friends and others about God?
What will you tell people?

PROPHECIES

Look up and chat about things Isaiah told about the coming of the Messiah:
His birth: Isaiah 7:14; 9:6
His family: Isaiah 11:1
Power from the Holy Spirit: Isaiah 11:2
Suffering and death: Isaiah 53
Future glory: Isaiah 11:3-16; 32:1

THE FUTURE

God showed Isaiah some future events, like a party on a mountain.
Who knows the future?
Why does God let us know some things about the future?

Travel Time

Let's go forward in the time tunnel to Matthew 26:67. *Wop, wop, wop!* Everything Isaiah said about Jesus being spit on and hit came true!

Chat about how sad it is for someone to spit and hit another person.

Matthew 26:67 Then they spit in his face and struck him with their fists. Others slapped him.

Journal Time

Draw a picture or write about the party on top of the mountain.

Prayer Time

Father God, thank You for letting us know about the future party and how animals will even get along together! Thank You for choosing strong people to be Your workers and messengers. Help us be brave so we will tell others about You. Amen.

22 Other Prophets and Messages

God sent many prophets to Israel. They gave messages from God. The prophets had a tough job. God sent them when the people disobeyed. The people put prophets in prison and killed some of them.

People called Jeremiah the weeping prophet because he cried for God's people. He taught with objects.

A ruined belt showed how useless the people were to God.

A potter shaping pots showed how God controls the shapes of lives and can destroy His creations.

A book sunk in a river showed that Babylon would be destroyed.

"Boohoo!" Jeremiah cried when he saw Babylonians capture Israel, as his visions had shown.

The prophet Joel spoke to Israel after locusts ate all their plants. He said God sent the bugs to warn them things would be worse unless they repented. Joel said an enemy army would take their land. He also said someday God would pour out His Holy Spirit on all people.

The prophet Hosea warned Israel to stop worshiping false gods. He said the Assyrians

would capture them. Hosea's wife ran away and ended up as a slave. Hosea bought her back and still loved her. God used this as a picture that the Messiah would still love and buy back His people even though they turned from God.

Micah said Israel and Judah would fall. He said God was angry with bad priests, dishonest leaders, and everyone believing false prophets. He told them to act justly, love mercy, and walk humbly with God. Micah predicted the Messiah's birth in Bethlehem seven hundred years before it happened! Wow!

Some prophets told what would happen to countries who hurt God's people. Obadiah said God would judge the Edomites, descendants of Esau. They helped armies attack Israel and stole property from Israel. Years later all the Edomites died.

Another prophet, Nahum, predicted that the Assyrians would fall.

Ezekiel, a prophet captured by Babylonians, told his imprisoned countrymen to be sorry for disobeying, so God would rescue them. He prophesied they would not be freed but one day God would gather His people together again. Ezekiel said the Messiah would be a good shepherd to His people.

The prophet Amos told people about two visions. One showed God destroying Israel's land with locusts and fire. Another showed that God's people were like a bowl of fruit, once beautiful but now rotten. He told the people not to trust their own power but to trust God.

Haggai, Zechariah, and Malachi were the last prophets. Israelites were now back in their own land. The prophets cheered the people on to rebuild the temple and prepare for the Messiah's coming. They reminded people of God's love and His promise to send a Savior.

Hello.
It's me, Daniel. You've heard about Elijah, Elisha, Jonah, and Isaiah.
You'll learn about me soon, but now it's time to explore other prophets and their messages.
- *Find out how a potter helped Jeremiah learn about God.*
- *Discover how God compared people to fruit.*

Chat Time

Chat Word: *Prepare* means to get ready. The prophets told the people to prepare for the Messiah's coming. ***How do we prepare for Christ's return?***

PREPARED

Are you prepared for Jesus to come today?

How do you feel about Jesus coming back?

GOD'S PROMISES

God promises to love and help those who obey Him.

How does God keep His promise?
Do you want to obey God?

HOPE

When you are sad and things go wrong, what helps?
Hope is to expect future good. What do you hope for?
Does knowing God will care for you help give you hope?

Travel Time

Let's go forward in the time tunnel to Matthew 2:1. *Wop, wop, wop!* Jesus was born in Bethlehem! **Look up the prophecy in Micah 5:2 and chat about how only God could have known this would happen.**

Matthew 2:1 After Jesus was born in Bethlehem in Judea, during the time of King Herod, Magi from the east came to Jerusalem.

Let's go forward again in the time tunnel, to Matthew 2:14-15. *Wop, wop, wop!* Jesus was called out of Egypt! **Look up the prophecy in Hosea 11:1 and chat about how only God could know this, too.**

Matthew 2:14-15 So he got up, took the child and his mother during the night and left for Egypt, where he stayed until the death of Herod. And so was fulfilled what the Lord had said through the prophet: "Out of Egypt I called my son."

Journal Time

Write or draw about how you feel when you are waiting for something special.

Prayer Time

How wonderful that You know all things, Lord. Help us be prepared for Your return. Amen.

23 Daniel, a Faithful Prophet

Bible Time Daniel

Alas! The Babylonians captured Israel. They took many people to Babylon as slaves. Their king, Nebuchadnezzar, chose Daniel and others to work in the palace. He gave them idol names of Belteshazzar for Daniel and Shadrach, Meshach, and Abednego for Daniel's three friends.

God gave Daniel and his friends wisdom and protected them. When Daniel's friends refused to bow to a statue of the king, soldiers threw them into a fiery furnace. Hot fire killed the soldiers, but God saved Daniel's friends. The king saw someone in the furnace with them.

God made Daniel wise and able to understand dreams. Wow! Daniel said one of King Nebuchadnezzar's dreams showed kingdoms that would come after the king's rule. Nebuchadnezzar told Daniel to help him understand the dream although it upset Daniel.

In the dream, a tree grew very tall, with green leaves and fruit.

A messenger called, "Cut it down and leave only a stump. Let the man be like a cow."

Daniel said the king would lose his mind and kingdom for seven years and live like a cow, eating grass, because he did not honor God. It happened!

King Nebuchadnezzar's hair grew to the ground, and his fingernails looked like bird's claws. After seven years the king became well, honored God, then ruled again.

Belshazzar became the next king. He gave a big party and used gold cups taken from God's temple in Jerusalem. Oh, no! A human finger wrote a message on the palace wall but only Daniel understood it!

God sent the message because the king worshiped idols. The words "Mene, Mene, Tekel, Parsin" meant God numbered the king's days, the king failed God's test, and his kingdom would be divided.

That night Darius, the Mede, killed King Belshazzar and became the new king.

Daniel was thrown into a lion's den for praying to God instead of the king. God saved Daniel. Daniel prophesied about rebuilding the wall of Jerusalem. He said the Messiah would come 476 years after the decree to rebuild the wall.

Daniel saw visions, too. He saw four beasts showing future kingdoms. He saw the most terrible kingdom destroyer. He also saw the Son of Man coming on a cloud.

Daniel dreamed of war. He cried for weeks, asking God to help him understand. An angel came, explaining God answered the first day but an evil being kept him from coming until the angel Michael helped. He told Daniel about many wars until the end of time. He also said that everyone whose name is written in the book will be saved, and they will shine like the stars. He said the rest would stay secret until the end of time.

Hello again!
Today you'll hear all about me, Daniel! I interpreted dreams, saw visions, and told people about the Messiah's coming.

- *Find out who wrote on a wall.*
- *Discover why God's answer took so long to get to Daniel.*

Chat Time

Chat Word: *Faithful* means to live by the rules you believe. Daniel was faithful to God's rules. Chat about how we need to first know God's rules before we can live them.

FAITHFULNESS

Daniel followed God in a palace where kings worshiped idols.
Is it hard to follow God when other people don't?

How can you follow God today?

CHURCH

GOD'S PROTECTION

God protected Daniel and his friends from fire and lions.
How does God protect you?

How do you get your name in God's book?

SHINING STARS
Who did God say would shine like the stars?

Travel Time

Let's go forward in the time tunnel to Matthew 24:15. *Wop, wop, wop!* Jesus is saying that what Daniel wrote is about the future and will come true.

Chat about how many prophecies in the Bible have not yet happened.

Matthew 24:15 "So when you see standing in the holy place 'the abomination that causes desolation,' spoken of through the prophet Daniel—let the reader understand."

Journal Time

Draw or write about being shining stars.

Prayer Time

Dear Father, thank You for sending faithful men like Daniel. It is wonderful to know You can protect us anywhere and from any harm! Help us be faithful. Amen.

24 Nehemiah, a Rebuilder

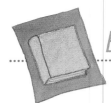

Hello!

My name is Esther and I'm your new tour guide. I lived in a palace during my people's captivity in Persia.

- *Find out how Nehemiah helped my people rebuild our holy city.*
- *Find out how many days it took to rebuild the wall.*
- *Discover Nehemiah's plan that helped the people keep working.*

Many Israelites stayed captive in strange places. Nehemiah, an Israelite, served Persian king Artaxerxes. He tasted and served the king's drinks to make sure the drinks contained no poison.

When Nehemiah heard about problems in Jerusalem, he cried for days. He prayed and fasted, asking God to forgive His people and let him help.

The king asked why Nehemiah looked sad.

Nehemiah said, "My people's city is broken. The wall is a pile of rocks and fire burned the gates. It's been a pile of rubble for seventy years!"

King Artaxerxes sent Nehemiah to rebuild the wall. He also gave Nehemiah wood from his forest. Nehemiah rode into Jerusalem at night then checked the walls. He couldn't even get through some places because of the mess! Rocks had tumbled into piles and heaps.

Nehemiah called the people together. He said, "Come, let us rebuild Jerusalem's walls. God is with us."

Everyone worked in groups, rebuilding parts of the wall. They repaired the twelve gates, all named after things, such as sheep, fish, dung, fountain, water, horse, and east. They fixed the walls between the gates, too. They worked hard but trouble came.

Enemies named Sanballat and Tobiah teased them and planned an attack. The people cried and wanted to give up.

Nehemiah said, "Don't be afraid. Remember God is awesome!" Nehemiah also gave the people a great plan. Half the men worked with swords in their belts. Other men held spears and stood guard. It worked!

Then poor people complained. They had no money left for food. People had sold their fields and even their children to rich people.

At a big meeting, Nehemiah said, "This is not right! You lend money then charge high fees, so high that the poor will never be able to pay it back. Give them back their fields and stop charging for loans."

"We will do it," the rich said.

And the people all said, "Amen."

Enemies tried to trick Nehemiah into entering the temple, although he was not a priest. They warned him they would tell the king the Israelites were plotting a war. Nehemiah didn't fall for those tricks.

Hooray! The people finished rebuilding the wall in fifty-two days and made Jerusalem safe again!

Nehemiah knew the people needed to rebuild their faith. After the seventy years of being prisoners, they had forgotten God's words. They needed to remember they were in God's family. They listed each family's name.

Ezra, the spiritual leader, called the people together and read God's law. The people wept and asked God to forgive them.

Then the Israelites held a party and celebrated. Nehemiah helped them choose temple workers. They gave the walls to God in a ceremony, called a dedication. How wonderful!

Chat Time

Chat Word: *Rebuild* means to put back together something that broke.
Chat about how sometimes we need to rebuild friendships.

REBUILDING

When your room or something else becomes a mess, is it hard to fix?

What helps you keep working when you want to give up?

TEASING

Why does teasing hurt?
What can you do when someone teases you?

REMEMBERING GOD

How can we remember God's laws?
Why do we need to remember God's laws?

TEAMWORK

Why does it help to work with other people?
Does it help to pray in teams, too?

DEDICATE

The people dedicated their work to God.
What does dedicate mean?
Chat about how we can dedicate what we do by doing it for God.

Travel Time

Let's go forward in the time tunnel to Daniel 9:25. *Wop, wop, wop!* This prophecy is about the walls being rebuilt and the time of Christ's coming. **Chat about how God knew when the people would rebuild the wall.**

Daniel 9:25 "Know and understand this: From the issuing of the decree to restore and rebuild Jerusalem until the Anointed One, the ruler, comes, there will be seven 'sevens,' and sixty-two 'sevens.'"

Let's go forward again. *Wop, wop, wop!* In John 10:7, Jesus calls Himself the sheep gate. The city gates had names, and each meant something. **Talk about how Jesus is a sheep gate, and we are the sheep.**

John 10:7 Therefore Jesus said again, "I tell you the truth, I am the gate for the sheep."

Journal Time

Write or draw about the wall.

Prayer Time

Father, how wonderful to know You are with us when we work. Thank You for good, wise leaders. Help us not to be afraid when people tease us about being Christians. Amen.

25 Esther, a Woman Who Helped Her People

Bible Time Esther

Esther, a beautiful orphan, lived in Susa with her uncle Mordecai. One day Xerxes, the king of Susa, sent Queen Vashti away for being bad. Xerxes searched for a new queen and chose Esther.

King Xerxes gave a party honoring Esther. Mordecai found out two guards planned to kill the king. He told Esther, who told the king. The king discovered the plan was true and had the men killed.

King Xerxes chose Haman to be his trusted leader. King Xerxes said people must bow to Haman, but Mordecai would bow only to God, not to a man. Haman hated Mordecai and the Jewish people. Oh, what an evil man! Haman tricked the king into making a law to kill all

Jewish people on a certain day. Haman even made a hanging pole for Mordecai.

When Mordecai heard the law, he tore his clothes and cried for days. Many Jews cried and fasted. Mordecai told Queen Esther about the law and said she must talk to the king. Oh, no! If she went to the king without being called, he could kill her!

Esther felt scared. Mordecai said she would be safe if the king held out his gold rod, called a scepter. He said living in the palace would not keep Esther safe. Mordecai believed their people would be saved somehow and maybe this problem was the reason she became queen.

Esther asked her people to go without food for three days. She fasted, too. On the third day, Esther dressed in beautiful robes and walked to the king's hall. The king was so happy to see Esther that he held out his scepter. He asked what she wanted and offered her anything, even half his kingdom.

Esther said, "Please come to dinner and bring Haman." The king agreed.

At dinner, Esther asked King Xerxes to come to dinner again the next night with Haman. Haman felt so proud! He told everyone about the invitation. That night the king remembered Mordecai had saved his life, so he asked Haman how to honor someone. Haman thought the king would honor him.

Instead the king used Haman's ideas to honor Mordecai. Haman put a robe on Mordecai and led him around town, on horseback, shouting, "The king honors this man."

At the second dinner, Esther asked the king to save her life from an evil man. The king was angry that someone would hurt his queen. He asked, "Who would do such a thing?"

She said, "Haman." The king had Haman hung from his own hanging pole. He made Mordecai the new leader and made a new law that saved the Jewish people. They made the day they were saved a holiday called Purim.

Hello, I'm Esther.
Once, I was afraid to speak up for God's people, but I'm glad I did. Here's my story about what happened.

- *Find out how the king honored the man who saved his life.*
- *Discover how I could see the king and not die.*

Chat Time

Chat Word: *Save* means to protect or keep from harm.
Chat about what Jesus did to save people.

FASTING

Fasting, which is going without eating, is done as part of serious praying.
Have you ever fasted?
Do you think it helped for the people to fast?

DANGER

Esther was willing to die to save her people.
What can you do to show that life is important?

Have you ever been saved from danger?
Who should you talk to when you think someone wants to hurt you?

CELEBRATING LIFE

The Jews celebrate Purim to remember God saved their lives.
How can you celebrate to show that life is important?
Talk about why you are happy for the life of each person in your family.

Travel Time

Let's go back in the time tunnel to Exodus 1:22. *Pow, pow, pow!* Another leader tried to kill all the baby boys of God's people.
Chat about how God saved Moses at that time.

Exodus 1:22 Then Pharaoh gave this order to all his people: "Every boy that is born you must throw into the river, but let every girl live."

Let's go forward in the time tunnel to Matthew 2:16. *Wop, wop, wop!* Oh, no! Herod heard about Jesus and tried to have all babies killed so Jesus would be killed.
Chat about how Herod tried to kill Jesus.

Matthew 2:16 When Herod realized that he had been outwitted by the Magi, he was furious, and he gave orders to kill all the boys in Bethlehem and its vicinity who were two years old and under.

Journal Time

Write about or draw a picture of Queen Esther.

Esther Uncle Mordecai Queen Esther Esther and King Xerxes

Prayer Time

Thank You, Father, for keeping us safe. Help us trust You and not be afraid to help save the lives of other people. Amen.

26 Mary, a Willing Servant

Bible Time Luke 1:26-56

"Hello, favored one, the Lord is with you!" the angel Gabriel said. This surprised Mary.

God sent the angel Gabriel to bring Mary a very special message. Mary lived in the little town of Nazareth and was engaged to a man named Joseph. Mary and Joseph were both Israelites from the family of King David.

God's people knew that someday a descendant of David would have God's special baby, One who would be the Savior. But the angel's words puzzled Mary.

The angel spoke again, "Don't be afraid, Mary. God is happy with you. He chose you to have a baby boy. Name him JESUS. This child will be great. He will be called the Son of the Most High. God will give Him the throne of David, and His kingdom will last forever."

Wow! What an important message! But it was hard to understand.

Mary asked, "How can this happen? I am a virgin and not married. I have never slept with a husband like a wife does to have a baby." Gabriel said, "The Holy Spirit will come to you, and God's shadow will come over you. The baby will be special, the Son of God."

The angel gave Mary more news, "Your relative, Elizabeth, is going to have a baby soon. She is so old that no one thought she could have a baby, but nothing is impossible for God."

Mary answered, "I am God's servant. May it all happen as you say."

Hooray! Mary said yes!

Then the angel left. What a wonderful message!

Mary hurried to visit Elizabeth, who lived far away in the hills. When Mary greeted

Hello.

I'm Elizabeth. I'm the mother of John the Baptist. You'll hear about John later. You are entering a new time zone, the New Testament. Today let's explore what happened when an angel visited Mary.

- *Find out who surprised Mary.*

- *Discover what Elizabeth's baby did when Mary visited.*

Elizabeth, something wonderful happened. The baby growing inside Elizabeth jumped, and the Holy Spirit filled Elizabeth! She felt so much joy!

Elizabeth shouted, "Blessed are you and your baby! Why has the mother of my Lord come to see me? My baby jumped within me at the sound of your voice. You have believed God, and He will carry out His words."

Mary sang out, "My spirit rejoices in God, my Savior. My soul glorifies the Lord. He knows I do not think I am special. But God has done great things, and now all people will call me blessed. Holy is His name." Mary spoke about the greatness of God and His great mercy.

Mary praised God for remembering His people and His promise. She praised God for His kindness to the poor and His mercy to people who believe in Him and fear Him.

Mary and Elizabeth had a wonderful visit. Mary stayed for three months until it was almost time for the birth of Elizabeth's baby.

Chat Time

Chat Word: *Favored* means to be approved or specially chosen.
Chat about why the angel greeted Mary by calling her "favored one."

GOD'S PLANS

God's plans for Mary were very special.
Do you know that God has plans for you, too?

Are you ready to say "yes!" to whatever God wants you to do?

THE JUMPING BABY

Elizabeth felt her baby jump inside her.
Talk about how babies inside a mom grow and move.
Does your mom remember when you first jumped?

FAVORED

Chat about how being favored is not the same as being the favorite one.
Talk about how each person in your family is special.
Chat about how each child is special to God.

SHARING JOY

Elizabeth and Mary shared the joy of having babies.
Have you ever shared happy news with someone?
Chat about a time your family shared good news together.

Travel Time

Let's go back in the time tunnel to Isaiah 7:14. *Pow, pow, pow!* The prophet Isaiah, hundreds of years before Mary lived, prophesied that a virgin would give birth to the Savior.

Chat about how the name Jesus means Savior and that Jesus was also called Immanuel, which means "God is with us."

Isaiah 7:14 Therefore the Lord himself will give you a sign: The virgin will be with child and will give birth to a son, and will call him Immanuel.

Journal Time

Write or draw about the angel speaking to Mary.

MARY:
- was surprised
- was in awe of God
- was a servant of God
- loved God

Prayer Time

God, You are so wonderful! How great to send Jesus to be with us. How wonderful to choose Mary, someone willing to say "yes!" Help us say "yes!" to Your plans. Amen.

27 Elizabeth and John the Baptist

Bible Time Luke 1; John 1

Such an exciting day! Everyone in town rejoiced that God had finally blessed Elizabeth and Zechariah with a baby. When he was one week old, everyone came to see him and name him after his father.

But Elizabeth said, "We will name him John."

The people murmured, "That's not right. No one in your family has that name."

Zechariah had not spoken one word in nine months. He waved his arms for a writing tablet and wrote, "His name is John." Immediately, Zechariah could speak again!

Then people learned more about the mystery of John's birth. Zechariah was a priest and had been in the temple when the angel Gabriel came to him. Zechariah felt scared at seeing the angel.

Gabriel said, "Don't be afraid. God heard your prayer. Your wife, Elizabeth, will have a son. Name him John. He will be great in God's eyes. Never let him drink wine. He will be filled with the Holy Spirit. He will prepare people for the Lord's coming."

Well, Zechariah couldn't believe the news. He asked, "How can I be sure of this? My wife and I are old."

The angel answered, "I am Gabriel. I stand in God's presence. Because you did not believe my words, you will be silent until all this happens." The angel left. People worried because Zechariah stayed in the temple so long. When he came out he could not speak. Everyone believed he had seen a vision.

After he named John and could speak, the Holy Spirit filled Zechariah. He began praising God. This amazed everyone!

Zechariah said, "Praise God! The Lord has come to save His people!" He looked at his son and said, "My son, you will be God's prophet. You will teach the people about forgiveness and God's mercy."

John grew and lived in the desert. He wore clothes made from camel's hair and ate honey and locusts.

The prophet Isaiah wrote that God would send His messenger before He sent the Messiah. The messenger would be a voice calling from the desert, "Prepare the way for the Lord."

John baptized people in the Jordan River. People came and confessed their sins. John said he baptized with water, but the One coming after him would baptize with the Holy Spirit. This amazed people. It also confused some people. The priests asked who John was.

He answered, "I am not the Christ."

So, they asked, "Are you Elijah?"

"I am not," John said.

"Are you the Prophet?" they asked.

He said, "No."

They asked, "Who are you?"

John answered, "I am the voice calling in the desert, 'Make straight the way of the Lord.'"

John looked and waited for Jesus.

Hello again!

Elizabeth here! Today you'll learn more about my special son, John. God chose John to help people get ready for Jesus.

- *Find out what John ate in the desert.*
- *Discover how my husband and I knew what to name our son.*

Chat Time

Chat Word: A *messenger* is someone who delivers the words of another person.
Chat about how John the Baptist was a messenger.

JOHN'S BIRTH

Why did people notice John's birth?
Chat about your names and how they were chosen.

Hannah Josiah David Amy

ZECHARIAH'S WORDS

What did Zechariah say John would teach people?

Why do you think Zechariah praised God?

When have you wanted to praise God?

PREPARING FOR JESUS

What did John have people do to be ready for the Messiah?

Are you ready for Jesus to come again?

Travel Time

Let's go back in the time tunnel to Isaiah 40:3. *Pow, pow, pow!* We find Isaiah speaking about John the Baptist hundreds of years before it happened.

Chat about how amazing it is that God told His prophets so much about the future.

Isaiah 40:3 A voice of one calling: "In the desert prepare the way for the LORD; make straight in the wilderness a highway for our God."

Journal Time

Write or draw about John growing up in the desert.

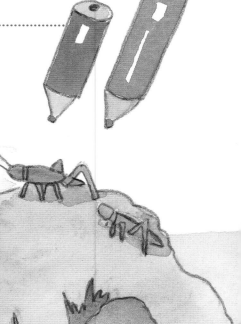

Prayer Time

Thank You, Father, for giving us so much proof that Jesus is Your Son. Help us believe Your messages. Amen.

28 The Birth of Jesus

Bible Time Matthew 1–2; Luke 1–2

Mary and Joseph planned to get married. Then Joseph found out about Mary's baby but knew he wasn't the father. He wondered if he should forget about marrying her.

Joseph went to sleep before doing anything. God sent an angel into Joseph's dream, who said, "Don't be afraid. Take Mary as your wife. This baby is from God's Holy Spirit. He is coming to save His people."

Wow! What a message! Joseph felt better. Joseph took Mary home and married her. When it came closer to the time for the baby's birth, the leader of the country, Caesar Augustus, made a new law.

The rule said every man needed to be counted in his own town. That meant people had to go wherever their families started long ago. Joseph and Mary left Nazareth and traveled to Bethlehem to be counted.

The day came for the birth of Mary's baby. Oh, no! They needed a place to stay but couldn't find any room. At last, an innkeeper let them use a stable with an animal feed box, called a manger. Mary gave birth to Jesus, wrapped him in cloths, and laid him in the manger.

That night, in fields near Bethlehem, some shepherds watched their sheep. God sent an angel to the shepherds. The angel appeared in the sky, and God's glory shone brightly around the shepherds. Oh! They were so scared! They shook with fright.

The angel said, "Don't be afraid. I have

great news! Today in Bethlehem, the city of King David, a baby was born. He is Jesus, the Christ, and He came to save you. You'll find Him lying in a manger."

Suddenly the sky filled with angels who cheered and sang, "Glory to God. Peace on earth to men of good will."

The shepherds hurried to Bethlehem and found the baby just as the angel had said. They told everyone they saw about the special baby.

Sometime later wise men, called Magi, came to Jerusalem looking for the child. They asked everyone, "Where is the new king? We saw His star in the East."

King Herod heard about the Magi.

His priests and teachers told him that the prophet said, "Out of Bethlehem will come a ruler to shepherd my people Israel."

King Herod held a secret meeting with the Magi. He found out when they first saw the star. He sent them to Bethlehem, making them promise to return with their news about the king.

The Magi found the star again and followed it to Jesus. They worshiped Him and gave Him gifts of gold, incense, and myrrh. They went home a different way, because a dream warned them not to see Herod again.

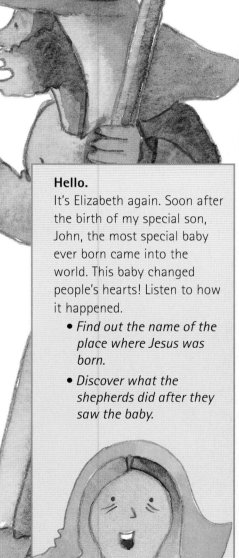

Hello.
It's Elizabeth again. Soon after the birth of my special son, John, the most special baby ever born came into the world. This baby changed people's hearts! Listen to how it happened.

- *Find out the name of the place where Jesus was born.*
- *Discover what the shepherds did after they saw the baby.*

Chat Time

Chat Word: *Savior* means someone who will rescue people.
Chat about what Jesus did as our Savior.

THE BABY
What was special about Jesus?

ROOM FOR JESUS

Do you have room for Jesus in your heart, in your life?
Why do you think God let Jesus be born in a little stable?

Chat about how each person in your family was born.

THE WISE MEN

Are you like the wise men, worshiping Jesus after finding Him?

They gave Jesus treasures. What do you think Jesus wants you to give Him?

THE SHEPHERDS

What do you think it looked like to see the glory of God?

Are you like a shepherd, telling everyone you meet about Jesus?

Travel Time

Let's go back in the time tunnel to Micah 5:2. *Pow, pow, pow!* The prophet Micah said Jesus would be born in Bethlehem.
Chat about how God always knows the future.

Micah 5:2 But you, Bethlehem Ephrathah, though you are small among the clans of Judah, out of you will come for me one who will be ruler over Israel.

Let's go back even further in time, to Genesis 49:10. *Pow, pow, pow!* God's Word said Jesus would be from the tribe of Judah.
Chat about Judah being a son of Jacob.

Genesis 49:10 The scepter will not depart from Judah, nor the ruler's staff from between his feet, until he comes to whom it belongs and the obedience of the nations is his.

Journal Time

Write or draw about the birth of Jesus and also about your own birth.

Prayer Time

Dear Father, thank You for sending Jesus as our Savior. Wow! How great it was to send angels to tell people about His birth! Help me to always have room in my heart for Jesus. Amen.

Bible Time Luke 2

Mary and Joseph wanted to follow God's laws about babies. So they brought Jesus to the temple when He was eight days old and presented Him to the priest. They also obeyed the law of giving thanks for the baby by offering two doves to God.

The Holy Spirit told Simeon, an old man, to go to the temple that day. He lived in Jerusalem, loved God, and obeyed God's commandments. The Holy Spirit had promised Simeon that he would see the Messiah before he died.

Simeon took Jesus in his arms and praised God, saying, "My eyes have seen Your salvation. He will be a light to the people who are not Jews, and He will bring glory to Israel."

Hooray! He knew Jesus was the promised Messiah!

Simeon's words amazed Mary and Joseph. Simeon told Mary, "This child will be a sign that will be spoken against. He will cause some to fall and others to rise. A sword will pierce your soul."

A very old widow at the temple, Anna, came up to them, too. She spent her days praying and worshiping God. She even went without food to pray more. She thanked God when she saw Jesus. She began telling everyone who looked for the Messiah news about Jesus.

Mary and Joseph took the

Hello.

My name is Matthew. Jesus chose me, a tax collector, to be a follower called a disciple. I wrote good news, called a Gospel, to tell people about Jesus. Today you'll find out what happened when Mary and Joseph took baby Jesus to the temple.

- *Find out why Simeon went to the temple and saw Jesus.*

- *Discover why Joseph took Mary and Jesus to Egypt.*

baby home. After the wise men's visit, an angel spoke to Joseph in another dream. He told Joseph to leave that night for Egypt because Herod wanted to kill Jesus. Joseph woke up Mary and they left with Jesus.

Soon, King Herod discovered that the wise men had tricked him. He became so angry that he had soldiers kill all Jewish baby boys in Bethlehem. When Herod died, the angel told Joseph in another dream that it was safe to bring his family back to Israel.

Joseph, Mary, and Jesus moved to Nazareth. Jesus grew strong and wise. Every year, Mary, Joseph, and Jesus traveled to the temple in Jerusalem to celebrate Passover, a special holy day.

When Jesus was twelve, his parents couldn't find him on their trip home. Since they traveled with many relatives and friends, they thought Jesus was with them, but he wasn't! They returned to Jerusalem and searched for three days. How worried they must have been!

Finally, on the third day, they found Jesus in the temple sitting with the teachers. He listened and asked questions. Jesus' answers amazed the men.

Mary scolded Jesus, "Your father and I have been anxiously searching for you. Why did you treat us badly?"

Jesus answered, "Didn't you know I had to be in My Father's house?"

But Mary and Joseph did not understand. Jesus went home with His family and obeyed them.

Chat Time

Chat Word: *Dedicate* means to give or set apart for a special purpose. Jewish law said the first son needed to be dedicated to God. That meant the parents promised to teach the boy to serve God. ***Chat about how we can promise to serve God.***

CHAT ABOUT YOUR GOING TO CHURCH

Talk about your earliest memories of church.

Parents, talk about when you first brought your children to church.
Chat about the importance of going to church.

WORRIED PARENTS

Children, chat about when you did something that worried your parents.

Parents, talk about why you always want to know where your children are.

DEDICATED

Parents, chat about how you want your children to serve God.

Chat about ways to serve God and make a promise to do so.

Travel Time

Let's go back in the time tunnel to Isaiah 42:6. *Pow, pow, pow!* Isaiah said similar words about Jesus, long before His birth. **Chat about how Jesus is a light to the world.**

Isaiah 42:6 I, the LORD, have called you in righteousness; I will take hold of your hand. I will keep you and will make you to be a covenant for the people and a light for the Gentiles.

Journal Time

Write or draw about going to church.

Prayer Time

Thank You, Jesus, for being our light. Help us to serve You and help others know You. Amen.

30 The Baptism of Jesus

Bible Time Matthew 3; Mark 1; Luke 3; John 1

When John started baptizing people, Jesus was also grown up. John told people to prepare for the Messiah and said strange things about the future. He said the Messiah would gather His wheat into the barn but burn the chaff. One day Jesus walked to the Jordan River to be baptized. John looked up, saw Jesus, and tried to stop Him. John knew Jesus was holy and did not need to repent. He said, "You should baptize me instead."

Jesus said, "Allow it. It is right for us to follow all God's ways."

Splash! John baptized Jesus. As Jesus rose from the water, the skies opened up. The Spirit of God flew down in the form of a dove and rested on Jesus.

A voice from heaven said, "This is My beloved Son in whom I am well pleased." How amazing!

The next day, when Jesus passed by, John pointed to Jesus, saying, "Behold, the Lamb of God who takes away the sin of the world."

John said that Jesus lived before him. He also said that God had shown him how he would know the Messiah. God said John would see the Spirit of God come and rest on the Savior.

When two of John's disciples heard his words, they began following Jesus and stayed with Him that night. The next morning, one of the men, Andrew, went to find his brother, Simon, to bring him to Jesus.

Andrew and Simon were fishermen. Jesus came to them as they were throwing a fishnet into the sea. He said to the brothers, "Follow me. I will make you fishers of men."

Jesus turned and said to Simon, "I will call you Peter." That means rock.

The three walked along the sea of Galilee and saw the sons of Zebedee, John and James. Jesus called them, too, and they followed Him.

Jesus called Philip to follow Him, who told his friend Nathanael, "We have found the One the prophets wrote about. He is Jesus, from Nazareth!"

When Jesus saw Nathanael, He said, "There's a man who tells the truth and is not tricky."

Nathanael asked, "How do you know me?"

Jesus answered, "Before Philip found you, I saw you under the fig tree." Wow! That's where Nathanael had been but nobody had seen him there.

Nathanael said, "Teacher, You are the Son of God!"

Jesus said, "You will see much more than this. You will see the heavens open and angels come down on the Son of Man."

Jesus also found Matthew, a tax collector, sitting in a tax office. He said, "Follow me." Matthew rose and followed Jesus. Jesus chose other disciples, too.

Hello.
It's Matthew again. It's time to learn all about the baptism of Jesus. It's so important that three gospel writing friends and I all told about it.

- *Find out who baptized Jesus.*
- *Discover what God, the Father, and God, the Holy Spirit, did at the baptism.*

Chat Time

Chat Word: *Trinity* means three persons in one God.
Chat about how the three persons in one God are equal but different.

BAPTISM
Chat about how baptism is done in your church.

Parents, tell your children about your own baptism.

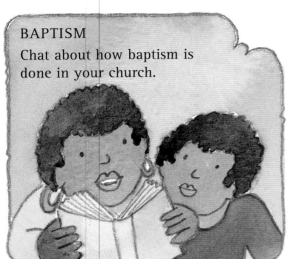

I am a disciple

I follow Jesus

JESUS

DISCIPLES
Chat about being a disciple of Christ.
Is it hard to follow Jesus all the time?

THE WHEAT AND THE CHAFF

What do you think it means that Jesus would gather the wheat?

What does it mean that He would burn the chaff, which is the useless outer shell of the wheat plant?

Travel Time

Let's go back in the time tunnel to Malachi 3:1. *Pow, pow, pow!* This prophecy told about John the Baptist coming before Jesus.

Chat about how John was the messenger who prepared people for Christ's coming.

Malachi 3:1 "See, I will send my messenger, who will prepare the way before me. Then suddenly the Lord you are seeking will come to his temple; the messenger of the covenant, whom you desire, will come," says the LORD Almighty.

Journal Time

Write or draw about Jesus' baptism.

Prayer Time

Thank You, Father, for sending John the Baptist. Thank You also for the people You sent in our lives to teach us about Jesus. Help us be good disciples. Amen.

31 The Wedding at Cana

Bible Time John 2:1-12

A wedding invitation came for Mary, the mother of Jesus. The family also invited Jesus and His friends, the disciples, to the wedding. It took place the day after Nathanael met Jesus.

After the wedding the groom (that's the man who got married) held a big party to celebrate. Hooray! A man and woman are married, and everyone is happy!

People called the man in charge of the party the master of ceremonies. Everyone drank wine and enjoyed the party. They were so thirsty that they drank all the wine, very fast.

Oh, how terrible to run out of drinks for the people at the party! Mary heard about the problem. She said to Jesus, "They have no more wine."

Jesus asked, "What difference does that make to you and me? It's not my time to do things."

But Mary turned to the servants and said, "Do whatever Jesus tells you to do."

Six huge stone water jugs stood near Jesus. The Jews had laws on washing hands before eating. These were called ceremonial laws. The jugs held water for the people to wash their hands in a special way, to follow these laws.

The jugs were big enough to hold twenty to

Hello.
My name is Mark. I wrote one of the Gospels and traveled with Paul and Barnabas to tell others about Jesus. Those great men helped me become a better follower of Jesus.

- *Find out who said Jesus would help with a problem.*
- *Discover what Jesus did to water.*

128

thirty gallons of water. That's about what a large garbage pail holds.

Jesus said to the servants, "Fill those jars with water."

Splish, splash! The servants poured water into all the jars until water reached the very tops.

Then Jesus said, "Dip some water out and bring it to the master of ceremonies."

The servants did what Jesus told them.

When the master of ceremonies took a sip and tasted the water, he tasted wine. It wasn't water anymore. The water had changed into wine! He didn't know where it came from, although the servants knew. He called the bridegroom to come see him.

The master of ceremonies said to the bridegroom, "Usually the person giving the party uses the best wine first. Then when people are full and don't care, they serve cheap wine that does not taste as good. But you saved the best wine until now!"

Wow! Jesus made wine better than the best wine at the party! He helped the bride and groom and solved the problem.

Changing water into wine was the first miracle Jesus did. All His disciples knew what happened and this made them believe in Him.

Weddings lasted several days. After the wedding in Cana ended, Jesus left and traveled to Capernaum for a few days. Mary, the brothers of Jesus, and the disciples went with Jesus. When Jesus left Capernaum He went to Jerusalem, the holy city. It was spring and time for the Passover celebration.

129

Chat Time

Chat Word: A *miracle* is when something happens that cannot be explained by science. ***Chat about the miracle of the water that became wine.***

PARTIES

Chat about inviting Jesus to your parties. Talk about any problems you've had at parties you gave.

BELIEVING IN JESUS

Chat about when and why the disciples believed in Jesus.

Why do you believe in Jesus?

When is the best time to believe in Jesus?

SAVING THE BEST

Is it good to save the best for last?

Should people try other religions and wait to try Jesus?

A MOTHER'S WORDS

Why do you think Mary asked Jesus to help?

Why did she tell the servants to listen when it sounded like Jesus didn't plan to help?

Talk about how your mother expects you to do things when you may not be ready.

Travel Time

Let's go forward in the time tunnel to Matthew 26:28. *Wop, wop, wop!* Jesus took wine, gave thanks, and said the wine was His blood. **Chat about what Jesus meant.**

Matthew 26:28 This is my blood of the covenant, which is poured out for many for the forgiveness of sins.

Journal Time

Draw or write about a wedding.

Prayer Time

Dear Lord, thank You for good times like parties. We are happy that You want to be with us when we celebrate. Help us believe in You. Help us also to listen to our mothers. Amen.

32 Feeding Five Thousand

Bible Time Matthew 14:13-21; Mark 6:30-44; Luke 9:10-17; John 6

Jesus and His disciples crossed the Sea of Galilee in a boat and found a quiet place to rest. People followed on land, running through towns, to be with Jesus. People brought sick friends and family. Jesus felt sorry for the sick, so He healed them. He taught about the kingdom of God all day long.

In the evening the disciples said, "We are far from towns. Send this crowd away so they can go eat and sleep."

Jesus answered, "Feed the people."

Philip cried out, "How can we? If a man worked eight months he would not earn enough money to feed this crowd."

Andrew, another disciple, said, "Here's a boy with his lunch to share. It's only five little loaves of barley bread and two fish. How far could that go?"

Jesus told His disciples to have the people sit on the green grass in big groups. After everyone sat, Jesus looked up to heaven, gave thanks, and broke the bread. He also divided the fish. The disciples gave bread and fish to everyone. They fed five thousand men plus women and children!

"Munch! Munch!" Every person ate until they were full.

Jesus said, "Gather the leftovers. Don't throw anything away."

The disciples filled twelve baskets with pieces of bread and fish.

Wow! Five little loaves of bread and two little fish fed a huge crowd, and the leftovers filled baskets!

When people saw this miracle they said, "He must be the prophet we've been waiting for."

Jesus sent the crowd home because He knew they wanted to make Him king. He sent

Hello.

I'm Mark, and I'm back to help you learn more about Jesus. Today you'll discover how He made a little bit of food go a long way in feeding many hungry people.

- *Find out who gave away his lunch.*
- *Discover what kind of bread Jesus said He would give people.*

His disciples out in the boat while He walked up a hill and prayed.

The next day people searched for Jesus. They didn't know He had walked on the water across the sea and met His disciples. They found Him on the other side of the lake.

Jesus said, "You looked for Me because I gave you bread. But that food goes bad. I have something better to give you."

"What does God want us to do?" the people asked.

"Believe in Me because the Father sent Me."

"Show us a sign, a miracle," the people said.

Jesus answered, "Long ago God sent bread from heaven called manna. It kept people alive. Now My Father wants to give you true bread from heaven. That's Me, for I am the Bread of Life."

The people did not understand.

Again Jesus said, "I am the Bread of Life. If you eat My flesh you will live forever."

Many left Jesus because they didn't understand. He asked the disciples if they wanted to leave, too.

"To whom would we go?" Peter asked. "You have the words of life. You are God's Son."

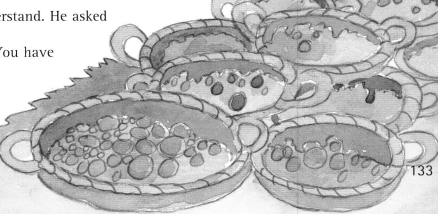

Chat Time

Chat Word: *Hunger* means to need food. It can also mean to need spiritual food. *Chat about people who need Jesus, the Bread of Life.*

IT'S A MIRACLE!

What did Jesus do before breaking the bread?

What should we do if we want a miracle?

HUNGER

What can you do to help people with hungry stomachs?

How can you help people who need Jesus?

SPIRITUAL FOOD

Chat about how Jesus is the Bread of Life.

What difference does Jesus make in your life?

What helps you to keep following Jesus?

FAITH

Why did some people walk away and leave Jesus?

Is it hard to understand or believe some things in the Bible?

Travel Time

Let's go forward in the time tunnel to
1 Corinthians 10:16. *Wop, wop, wop!*
Chat about communion at your church.

1 Corinthians 10:16 Is not the cup of thanksgiving
for which we give thanks a participation in the
blood of Christ? And is not the bread that we break
a participation in the body of Christ?

Journal Time

Draw or write about communion at your church.

Jesus the bread of life

Prayer Time

Thank You, Jesus, for giving us eternal life and for being our Bread of Life. Help
us to believe in You even when we do not understand. Help us to reach out to
others so they may have life that lasts forever, too. Amen.

135

33 Jesus Raises Jairus' Daughter

Bible Time Matthew 9:1, 18-26; Mark 5:21-43; Luke 8:40-56

Jesus rode the boat across the Sea of Galilee to His home town. Many people met Jesus there, for they had been waiting for Him.

"Please help my little girl!" cried a man. The man, a leader of the Jewish church, was named Jairus. He fell down in front of Jesus and knelt.

Jairus begged, "My daughter is dying, but if you come to my house and touch her, she will live!"

Jesus went with the man. Oh, no! Pushing and shoving, the crowd followed and almost crushed Jesus!

A sick woman in the crowd pushed closer to Jesus. She had spent all her money on doctors, but they didn't help her. For twelve years she had been bleeding, and still she kept bleeding. She grew sicker all the time.

She said to herself, "If I can touch His coat, I will be healed." The woman crept closer and closer. She reached and reached until she touched Jesus' coat.

Wow! As soon as her fingers touched the

Hello,
it's Mark again! Today you'll hear about a great miracle. This is one of my favorites!

- *Find out who touched Jesus as He was on His way to heal a girl.*
- *Discover why people laughed at what Jesus said.*

coat her bleeding stopped. She felt so much better!

Jesus felt power go out of Him and called out, "Who touched Me?"

People shook their heads, and everyone said, "It wasn't me!"

Peter said, "Master, the people are just pressing against You."

Jesus kept looking around, searching each face. The woman shook with fear and fell down at His feet. She told Jesus what she had done and why. She also told Him that touching His coat did heal her.

"Daughter, your faith healed you," Jesus said. "Go home now."

At that moment someone came from the home of Jairus, saying, "Your daughter is dead! Don't bother the teacher any longer."

Jesus turned to Jairus and said, "Don't be afraid. Believe and she will be healed."

Jesus walked on, but let only Peter, John, James, and the little girl's parents go with Him. When He came to the house He heard lots of noise. People were crying, and someone played a flute. The music meant someone had died.

Jesus told the flute player to go home. He said to the crowd, "Why are you making so much noise? Go away. The little girl is only asleep."

People laughed. They knew she was dead. Jesus went into the house. He took His disciples, Jairus, and the girl's mother with Him. He found the little girl in bed. She was twelve years old.

Jesus held the girl's hand and said, "Talitha koum!" That means "Little girl, get up!"

Pop! The little girl jumped up and walked around. This amazed everyone.

Jesus said, "Feed her." He told them not to talk about the miracle.

But the news of what happened spread to the whole area.

Chat Time

Chat Word: *Raise* means to lift up. Raising someone from the dead, called resurrection, means to bring a person back to life.
Chat about how Jesus will raise up all believers who die.

RESURRECTION

Chat about how all the believers you love will also be raised.
Chat about heaven and eternal life.

PRAYER ANSWERS

Talk about times when you wanted Jesus to answer a prayer so much.
How has Jesus answered some of your prayers?
Has He done miracles in your life?

TAKING TOO LONG

Did it seem Jesus took too long to help Jairus' daughter?

Does it seem that sometimes Jesus takes too long to answer your prayers?

Jesus told Jairus to believe when it seemed hopeless. Chat about something that seems hopeless and how you can still believe Jesus for an answer.

Travel Time

Let's go back in the time tunnel to Isaiah 26:19. *Pow, pow, pow!* The prophet Isaiah spoke about the resurrection, too.

Chat about why people will want to shout with joy at the resurrection.

Isaiah 26:19 But your dead will live; their bodies will rise. You who dwell in the dust, wake up and shout for joy. Your dew is like the dew of the morning; the earth will give birth to her dead.

Journal Time

Write or draw about someone you want to see again who died.

Prayer Time

Thank You, Jesus, for letting us be close to You. Help us not be sad when we wait for You to answer prayers. Amen.

34 The Beatitudes

Bible Time   Matthew 5; Luke 6

The disciples and many people came to Jesus to listen. One beautiful day Jesus climbed a mountainside and sat down to teach. People gathered around. Jesus said many wise things.

"Blessed are people who are mild, or humble, for the kingdom of heaven belongs to them."

"Blessed are people who cry because of a loss. They will feel better."

"Blessed are people who are gentle and think more of others than of themselves. They will be given the earth."

"Blessed are people who really want what is right. These people hunger for what is right in God's eyes. They will be satisfied."

"Blessed are people who are kind and forgiving, or merciful. They shall receive mercy."

"Blessed are people with clean, or pure, hearts, for they will see God."

"Blessed are people who help make peace, for they will be called God's children."

"Blessed are people whom others hurt and tease because they do what is right. They try to follow God. The kingdom of heaven belongs to these people."

"Blessed are you when others pick on you and hate you because of Me. They may tell evil lies about you and laugh at you. Rejoice! Be happy because God will give you a great reward in heaven. These are the same ways people hurt God's prophets."

Hi there!

My name is Luke. I was a doctor and a good friend of the apostle Paul. God gave me the words to write a gospel. Today you'll learn that Jesus told people to be blessed, or happy, even with problems. These are called Beatitudes.

- *Find out why you should be happy when people are mean to you.*
- *Find out how Jesus said to treat people.*
- *Discover what to do to your enemies.*

Jesus warned some people. He said, "Watch out, rich people, for you have already been comforted. Woe to people who feel well fed, for you will go hungry."

"People who laugh now, be careful for you will cry and be sad."

"Watch out if men say good things about you now, for that is how their fathers talked about false prophets who lied. Those were people who said God sent them when He did not."

Jesus spoke about what people who love God are like.

"You are like salt on earth. If salt loses its saltiness it cannot become salty again. It must be thrown away."

"You are like a light to this world. You cannot hide a city on top of a hill. You would not hide a light under a bed or under a bowl? No! You would put the light on a table to shine. Let your light shine so people can see it."

Jesus told people why He came. He said, "I came to fulfill the Law and words God gave the prophets. Every law from God is important. If you break the little laws you will be little in heaven. If you obey the laws you will be great in heaven."

Jesus also told people to do more than follow the laws. He said, "Treat people the way you want them to treat you. Love your enemies. Be good to people who hate you."

Chat Time

Chat Word: The *Beatitudes* are the statements Jesus made about blessing people who have problems.
Chat about how the blessings may come after the problems.

LISTENING

What Beatitudes did you listen to that made you feel better?

How do the Beatitudes help you feel good about the future?

Chat about the rewards Jesus told about in the Beatitudes.

BEING HUMBLE

Chat about what it means to be humble or mild.

How was Jesus humble?

Chat about Jesus being born in a humble place.

LOVING ENEMIES

Chat about praying for your enemies.

Chat about people who have hurt you on purpose.

How can you do good to people who hurt you?

LIGHT AND SALT

Chat about ways salt is used.
Chat about how light helps us.
How can you be salt or light for people?

SALT

Travel Time

Let's go back in the time tunnel to Isaiah 61:1-2. *Pow, pow, pow!* The prophet told how God would send Jesus to preach and bring comfort to people.
Chat about how Jesus comforts us.

Isaiah 61:1-2 The Spirit of the Sovereign LORD is on me, because the LORD has anointed me to preach good news to the poor. He has sent me to bind up the brokenhearted, to proclaim freedom for the captives and release for the prisoners, to proclaim the year of the LORD's favor and the day of vengeance of our God, to comfort all who mourn.

Journal Time

Write or draw about praying for someone who hurt you.

Prayer Time

Dear Lord, thank You for your words of comfort and hope. Help us hope when we are in pain. Help us love people who hurt us and give us clean hearts and a gentle spirit so we will be kind to all people. Amen.

35 The True Vine

Bible Time Matthew 7:14; John 15-16

Jesus told a story about growing grapes in a field called a vineyard. The grape gardener is called a vinedresser.

"Heaven is like a vineyard," Jesus said. "The owner of the vineyard looked for men to work in the vineyard one morning."

The owner hired men early in the morning. They agreed to work for one day's pay. Three hours later, the owner hired more workers. At noon, he hired more workers. In the middle of the afternoon, he hired a few more workers. About an hour before the workday ended the owner found men standing around.

"Why have you done nothing all day?" he asked.

The men said, "Because no one would give us a job."

He hired them to work for the one hour.

At the end of the day he gave everyone the same pay, a day's wages.

The men who started work early grumbled, "Grr, that's not fair. You paid the men who worked only one hour the same amount you paid us."

The owner said, "I paid you what we agreed upon. That's fair. And if I want to give everyone the same amount I can because it is my vineyard. Are you angry because I am generous?"

Another time Jesus spoke about where people pick grapes. He said, "You don't pick grapes from a thorn bush. You know where grapes grow."

He then told people they also can know what grows in a good person's heart by what that person does.

Not long before Jesus died He told His disciples that He is like a vine. Jesus said, "I am the true vine, and my Father is the vinedresser."

"Like a good gardener, the Father cuts away the bad parts of the vine where no fruit grows. He trims fruitful ones so they will grow even more fruit."

Then Jesus said, "I am the vine. That makes you the branches. Branches need to stay as part of the vine, or nothing grows on them. So, stay close to Me."

He explained, "You cannot do anything without Me. If you don't stay in Me you will be like a broken branch that dries up, dies, and is thrown away. Stay in Me, and you will be very fruitful and people will see what My Father is like."

Jesus said, "I love you the same way that My Father loves Me. Stay in My love. I obey My Father and stay in His love. Obey Me so that you will stay in My love."

Jesus said He calls people who keep His commands "friends." Then He added, "My command is that you love each other as I have loved you."

Hello!
It's Luke again! Today you'll learn how Jesus spoke about grapes and the vines that grapes grow on.

- *Find out what part of a vine you are like.*
- *Discover who Jesus calls a friend.*

Chat Time

Chat Word: A *vine* is a plant with a long stem that grows on the ground. Other stems, or branches, grow off the main stem.

Chat about what it means to belong to Jesus, the true vine.

BELONGING

Talk about how even the branches way out on a vine are still part of it.

Chat about how we belong to God's family.

Chat about having Jesus as your friend.

FRUITFUL

Chat about how many clusters of grapes grow on a vine.

How can you be fruitful, producing something sweet for others?

FAIR

Chat about how parents may not give each child exactly the same things because they have different needs.

LOVING OTHERS

How does Jesus love you?

How can you love people like Jesus does?

Travel Time

Let's go back in the time tunnel to Jeremiah 23:5. *Pow, pow, pow!* Jesus is called a special branch, a King.

Chat about the main branch of a vine on which the other branches grow and how long before His birth God gave Jesus this name.

Jeremiah 23:5 "The days are coming," declares the LORD, "when I will raise up to David a righteous Branch, a King who will reign wisely and do what is just and right in the land."

Journal Time

Draw or write about being part of the true vine.

Prayer Time

O Lord, thank You for calling us Your friends and for letting us belong to You. Bless us with growth and help us be fruitful. Amen.

36 Jesus Heals Lepers

Bible Time Exodus 4:6-7; Leviticus 13:39-46; Matthew 8:1-4, 10:8; Mark 1:39-42; Luke 4:27, 5:11-14, 7:22, 17:11-19

"No prophet is welcomed in his hometown. In the days of Elijah there were many lepers, but God healed only Naaman," Jesus said. Naaman followed the orders of Elijah and dipped himself in a river seven times and was healed.

The Israelite laws told people how to treat lepers. A leper had a disease that ate away his skin and caused much pain. It looked like a sore but went deep into the skin, and hair around it turned white. The laws called lepers unclean and stated that lepers had to walk around with their clothes torn. Lepers had to stay away from all healthy people. How sad to live away from family because of a sickness!

If the sores healed then a priest had to see the person and state that he was clean before that person could go home and be with family.

God even used leprosy as a sign to

show people that He chose Moses. When Moses touched his bare chest, his hand became leprous. When Moses touched his chest again, his hand was clean.

Jesus used the example of Elijah to tell people in His hometown, Nazareth, that He would not perform miracles there because they did not welcome Him.

Early in His work, Jesus healed many people. John the Baptist had asked if Jesus was the One they expected. Jesus told John's disciples to tell John about what He did, even that He healed lepers. The news showed that Jesus did what the prophets said He would do.

Jesus traveled around Galilee. Many people followed Jesus. In one of the cities a leper fell down before Jesus. He cried, "Lord, if You want You can make me clean!"

Jesus looked at the man and felt so sorry for him. Jesus reached His hand way out, touched the leper, and said, "I am willing. Be clean." At once the man's sores disappeared. Hooray! His leprosy was cleansed.

Jesus said, "Go and let the priest see you, but don't tell anyone what happened." But the news of the miracle spread everywhere. More people came and brought their sick to Jesus to be healed.

One time, when Jesus walked toward Jerusalem, ten lepers stood in the distance. "Jesus! Master!" they shouted. "Have mercy on us!"

Jesus simply said, "Go and let the priest look at you."

As the men started walking they were healed! One of them, a Samaritan, returned to Jesus.

That man knelt at the feet of Jesus and thanked Him.

Looking around, Jesus asked, "Didn't ten get healed? Where are the other nine? Did only the person from another country return?" Then He said to the Samaritan, "Get up. Your faith made you well."

Hello!

Luke here again! As a doctor I am amazed at how Jesus heals people. Today you'll learn how Jesus healed people of a terrible sickness. They were called lepers because of the sickness.

- *Find out how many lepers Jesus healed at one time.*
- *Discover how many of the lepers thanked Jesus for being healed.*

Chat Time

Chat Word: *Thankful* means to feel happy about what has happened and to know someone else helped it happen.
Chat about how being thankful also makes you feel happy.

THANKFULNESS

Chat about when God has healed you or someone else.
Let each person say one thing for which they are thankful.
Let each person tell one thing God made that makes them feel thankful.

FAITH

Why did Jesus say the leper's faith made him well?

Do you believe God will answer your prayers?

SPREADING NEWS

Chat about how the news of what Jesus did might have spread.
Do you tell others about the good things God has done for you?

Think of one thing God did for you that you will talk about to others.

Travel Time

Let's go back in the time tunnel to Psalm 147:3. *Pow, pow, pow!* This verse tells how God heals wounds.
Chat about how Jesus can heal us because He is God.

Psalm 147:3 He heals the brokenhearted and binds up their wounds.

Journal Time

Write or draw about someone who needs healing.

Prayer Time

Thank You, Jesus, for healing people. Help us remember to thank You when You answer our prayers. Amen.

37 A Sinful Woman Anoints Jesus

Bible Time Luke 7, 8:1-2; John 12:1-8

Many women listened to Jesus and helped pay for His needs with their money. Joanna, the wife of Chuza, helped. Her husband worked for Herod, a leader who worked for the Romans. Jesus had healed some of these women. He even cast seven demons out of Mary Magdalene.

One unnamed woman cared for Jesus in a special way. Simon, a Pharisee, invited Jesus to dinner. The woman came into Simon's home with expensive lotion in a beautiful box made of alabaster. Weeping, she stood behind Jesus. *Drip, drip,* tears fell on His feet. She bent down and washed His feet with her tears. She kissed His feet and dried them with her hair. She anointed Jesus' feet with the perfumed lotion. The sweet smell filled the house.

Simon and the other guests wondered, "How can He be a prophet? He doesn't even know this woman is bad!"

"Simon, let me tell you a story," Jesus said. He told about two men who owed money. One person owed a little bit, but the other owed a huge amount of money. Neither man could pay what he owed. The man who lent the money forgave them and said, "I won't make you pay back the money."

Jesus asked, "Which man will love the lender more?"

Simon answered, "The one who owed the most."

Hi again from Luke!
I thought you might like to know about women who met Jesus. You'll read about a few today.

- *Find out how women helped Jesus.*
- *Discover how a bad woman washed Jesus' feet.*

"Yes, he will be more thankful," Jesus said. "It's the same with this woman. You didn't wash My feet or kiss Me. She has not stopped caring for Me since she arrived. Her many sins are forgiven."

Men grumbled some more. "Who is this man to say He forgives sins?"

Jesus looked at her and said, "Go in peace, for your faith has saved you."

Just before the Passover celebration, Jesus ate at the home of Simon the leper. A woman named Mary came with an alabaster jar of perfume. Her brother, Lazarus, had once been dead but Jesus had brought him back to life. Lazarus was an invited guest at this meal.

Mary wept and washed Jesus' feet with her tears. She poured perfume over the feet and head of Jesus. Sniff! sniff! How sweet the whole house smelled.

Grumble! grumble! People felt angry about the woman and perfume.

The disciple Judas Iscariot asked, "Why waste this perfume? Why wasn't it sold and the money given to the poor?" Judas took care of the money for Jesus and the disciples. He didn't really care about the poor, for he stole money and used it for himself. Later Judas turned on Jesus and was no longer his friend.

Jesus said, "Leave her alone. You will always have poor people, but you will not always have Me. She is getting Me ready to be buried."

Chat Time

Chat Word: *Serve* means to do things for other people, even little things, like washing their feet.

Chat about ways to serve the people in your family.

SERVICE

How does your family serve Jesus with money?

How does your family serve people with their hands?

Can you choose one new way to serve God this week?

Who does Jesus want you to serve?

WHAT CAN JESUS DO?

What sins can Jesus forgive?

How do you thank Jesus for forgiving your sins?

Jesus was kind to the woman. How should you treat sinful people?

Thank You, Jesus, for forgiving.

FEET

Chat about how Jesus walked in sandals so His feet were very dirty.

Can you set a time to wash each other's feet and even massage them?

After washing feet, talk about how it felt.

Travel Time

Let's go forward in the time tunnel to John 13:14. *Wop, wop, wop!* Jesus washed the feet of His disciples to show them that no one is too great to serve other people.

Chat about how we are never too important to help in little ways.

John 13:14 Now that I, your Lord and Teacher, have washed your feet, you also should wash one another's feet.

Journal Time

Write or draw about washing someone's feet.

Prayer Time

Thank You for letting us serve You by helping the people You love. Thank You for forgiving all our sins. Help us be kind to all people. Amen.

38 Walking on Water

Bible Time

Matthew 14:22–32; Mark 4:35–41, 6:45–52;
Luke 8:22–25; John 6:16–21

Jesus taught a great crowd all day long. In the evening Jesus said to His close friends, the disciples, "Let's cross the lake." They all climbed in a boat and Jesus fell asleep.

The disciples rowed, but suddenly lightning flashed and thunder crashed around them. *Whish! whish!* The wind blew hard. *Splash!* Water started filling the boat. The water poured in and almost filled the boat. Jesus lay fast asleep in the back of the boat with His head resting on a pillow.

"Wake up, Teacher!" the disciples shouted. "Don't You care that we might drown?"

Jesus woke up, looked around, and called out to the wind, "Quiet!" The wind stopped blowing. The waves stopped crashing. Silence filled the air.

Jesus asked, "Why were you afraid? Don't you have faith in Me?"

This surprised the disciples. They said, "Who is this man? Why, even the wind and water listen and obey Him!"

That was not the only time the disciples fought a storm. Another time after teaching, Jesus sent His friends off in a boat while He climbed a hill to pray.

Splash! Swish! Waves crashed against the boat and the wind blew and rocked it up and down. Jesus had sent His special disciples in the boat, but He could see them from the top of a hill where He stood. Jesus saw his friends rowing hard.

They were rowing for the seashore, but the wind kept blowing them away from the shore.

In the middle of the night Jesus walked right on top of the water to reach His friends. Jesus looked like a ghost in the storm. The disciples shook with fear. They yelled and screamed.

"Be brave," Jesus said. "It is I. Do not be afraid."

"Lord, if it is You," called Peter, "tell me to come to You."

"Come!" Jesus said.

Peter hopped out of the boat. He put one foot on the top of the water, then his other foot, and took a step. Wow! He walked on top of the water. He didn't sink in the waves.

Oh, no! Peter stopped looking at Jesus. Peter looked at the waves and felt the swishing of the wind against his face. *Blop! Blop! Blop!* Peter began sinking in the waves.

"Help! Lord, save me!" Peter cried.

Jesus grabbed Peter's hand and caught Peter.

"Oh, Peter, you have so little faith. Why didn't you trust Me?" Jesus asked.

Jesus and Peter climbed into the boat. As they climbed aboard, the wind died and the waves stopped. The disciples looked around and saw the boat was almost where they had been rowing to, about three miles from where the boat had been tossing about in the storm!

Hello,

I'm Peter, your tour guide. I walked with Jesus and shared many adventures with Him. I even had a strange walk with Jesus that you'll hear about today.

- *Find out when Peter started to sink.*
- *Discover how Jesus stopped the storm.*

Chat Time

Chat Word: *Trust* means to be sure of another person and to believe in his or her ability. **Chat about trusting God during storms or earthquakes.**

PETER'S SHORT PRAYERS

What two short prayers did Peter say when he saw Jesus walk on water?

How did Jesus answer Peter's prayers?

What happens when you ask God to help you do something difficult?

Talk about how believing God will help you when you ask.

THE POWER OF JESUS

Can anyone tell the wind to stop?

How does this story show Jesus is more powerful than storms?

What would Jesus say if you cried, "Wake up, Lord, I have a problem!"

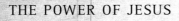

FAITH AND TRUST?

Do you believe God can do anything?

Do you trust that He will always help you?

Talk about a time Jesus did help you with a problem.

Travel Time

Let's go back in the time tunnel to Job 9:8. *Pow, pow, pow!* It says only God has power over the waves.
Chat about how Jesus calming the storms reminds us that Jesus is God the Son.

Job 9:8 He [God] alone stretches out the heavens and treads on the waves of the sea.

Journal Time

Write or draw about a storm that scared you.

Prayer Time

Dear Lord, You are so powerful. Help us trust in Your power and not be afraid of storms or scary things. Help our faith to grow. Amen.

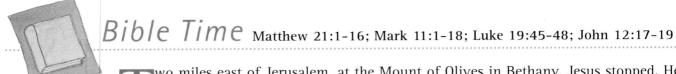

39 A Big Parade

Bible Time Matthew 21:1-16; Mark 11:1-18; Luke 19:45-48; John 12:17-19

Two miles east of Jerusalem, at the Mount of Olives in Bethany, Jesus stopped. He told two disciples, "Go to town. You'll find a donkey with her colt. Untie both and bring them to Me."

Jesus added, "If anyone asks, 'Why are you doing this?' say, 'The Lord needs it and will send it back.'"

The disciples found the animals tied at a doorway. The owners asked, "What are you doing?"

The owners let them go when the disciples repeated Jesus' words.

Clip clop! The donkey and colt trotted beside the disciples. When they came to Jesus, the disciples spread their coats on the colt, lifted Jesus up, and set Him on the colt.

This was exactly what the prophet Zechariah had said would happen!

Long before, Zechariah wrote, "Say to the daughter of Zion, 'See your king comes gently, riding on a donkey, on a colt, the baby of a donkey.'"

The disciples marched behind Jesus, beginning a parade. They joyfully shouted, praising God for miracles they had seen. Some people spread their coats on the road while others cut and laid down branches.

"Hosanna!" people shouted. "Blessed is He who comes in the name of the Lord! Hosanna in the highest!"

Some Jewish leaders, called Pharisees, stood nearby. They didn't like what they saw or heard. They yelled, "Teacher, tell Your disciples to stop!"

"If they stop," Jesus said, "the stones will shout."

When He saw Jerusalem, Jesus stopped. Tears rolled down His cheeks.

He said, "If only you knew what would bring peace today, but now it is hidden from your eyes."

Jesus prophesied, "Days will come when enemies will hurt you. They will surround and crush you. Not one stone will be left in place, because you did not understand this time of God's coming."

As Jesus went into Jerusalem, people asked, "Who is this?"

The crowd shouted, "He is Jesus, the prophet from Nazareth."

Jesus marched into the temple. It looked like a big store, not a place to worship God! People changed foreign coins for temple coins and sold doves and other things. They cheated the people, too! Jesus chased them away.

"It is written," Jesus said, repeating words of the prophet Jeremiah, "My house is called a house of prayer, but you made it a place of robbers."

This upset the head priests and temple teachers. They wanted to kill Jesus. They grumbled, "Humph! Everyone's following Him!"

Even children followed and sang, "Hosanna to the son of David!"

The priests asked, "Do you hear the children?"

Jesus answered, with words of a psalm, "From the mouths of children God has sent praise."

As the sun set, Jesus and His disciples went back to Bethany.

Shalom!
That's a Jewish word for peace. I'm John, your new tour guide. Jesus called me His beloved disciple, and that's what He wants to call you, too. Today you'll learn about a peaceful parade.

- *Find out what Jesus rode in the parade.*
- *Discover what words the people sang.*

Chat Time

Chat Word: *Praise* means to say words that show you know God is great. Let everyone say words of praise.

THE PARADE

Palm Sunday celebrates the day of this parade. It is also called the Triumphal Entry. Chat about what your church does on Palm Sunday.

The word hosanna means save. Why would the people yell save?

Kings rode donkeys in times of peace. Chat about why Jesus rode a donkey.

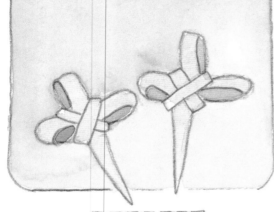

THE PROPHECY OF JESUS

What did Jesus say would happen to Jerusalem?

Forty years after Jesus died, His words came true. Enemies destroyed the temple and city and killed more than one million people in Jerusalem. Chat about why Jesus said this would happen.

BAD PEOPLE IN THE TEMPLE

Who did Jesus chase out of the temple? Why?

Does God care about His house, your church?

How should you behave in your church?

Travel Time

Let's go back in the time tunnel to Zechariah 9:9. *Pow, pow, pow!* Zechariah said Jesus would ride a donkey! **Chat about how God told the prophets so much about Jesus.**

Zechariah 9:9 Rejoice greatly, O Daughter of Zion! Shout, daughter of Jerusalem! See, your king comes to you, righteous and having salvation, gentle and riding on a donkey, on a colt, the foal of a donkey.

Journal Time

Draw or write about the parade.

Prayer Time

Thank You, Lord, that we know why You came. We rejoice and praise You, for You are our king. Amen.

40 The Last Supper

Bible Time Matthew 26:14-35; Mark 14:12-29; Luke 22:7-30; John 13:21-30

At last, the day of Passover came! Jesus sent His close friends, Peter and John, telling them, "Get everything ready to celebrate."

The disciples asked, "Where should we go?"

Jesus said, "When you enter Jerusalem you will see a man carrying a water jar. Follow him. When he enters a house find the owner and say, 'The teacher wants to know, "Where is the guest room where I may eat with My disciples?"'"

Jesus told Peter and John that the man would show them a large room in the upstairs of the house. Everything happened as Jesus had said! They prepared everything for the meal.

Evening came. Jesus and the disciples came into the room. Jesus looked at them and said, "I have really wanted to celebrate Passover with you before I suffer. I won't eat this again until it is fulfilled in God's kingdom."

When the hour to celebrate came, Jesus and His friends gathered around the table.

They could stretch out and lie back around the special table. While they ate, Jesus said, "One of you will turn Me over to enemies. It would have been better for him to never have been born."

This made the disciples sad. They each said, "It won't be me, Lord!"

Jesus answered, "I am dipping my bread in this bowl. The person who shares this bread is the one." Jesus dipped the bread and gave it to Judas Iscariot, son of Simon. Right away, Satan took control of Judas' heart.

Judas said, "Surely it is not I, Teacher."

Jesus looked at Judas and said, "Yes, it is you. Go and carry out your plans quickly." Judas left after taking the bread.

They continued to eat. Jesus lifted up bread and gave thanks. He broke the bread and gave it to His friends. He said, "Take this. It is My body. Do this to remember Me."

After supper, Jesus picked up His cup of wine and gave thanks.

Then Jesus said, "Drink from this cup. It is My blood. It is poured out to forgive sins. I won't drink fruit of the vine again until I drink with you in My Father's kingdom."

Then Jesus stood up, grabbed a towel, and put it around His waist. He poured water in a bowl then washed the feet of one disciple then another. He moved around the table and bent to wash Peter's feet.

But Peter cried, "I can never let You wash my feet!"

Jesus said, "Then you won't belong to Me."

"Then wash my hands and head, too!" Peter shouted.

"Only your feet need washing," Jesus said.

After this they sang a hymn and walked to the Mount of Olives.

Hosanna to God!
It's John again. What an exciting story I have today! It's about a special meal Jesus had with the disciples. That includes me because I'm a disciple.

- *Find out what Jesus did that servants do.*
- *Discover what Jesus did with bread at the meal.*

Chat Time

Chat Word: *Passover* is a day, once a year, to remember when God saved each firstborn son of Israel. Jesus and His disciples celebrated Passover three times.
Chat about how Jesus gave His life for us.

THE LAST SUPPER

Talk about how the house was ready for the disciples when they needed it.
Chat about how your church celebrates the Lord's Supper.
Chat about what Jesus said about bread being His body.

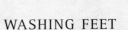

WASHING FEET

When you play outside in sandals or barefoot, do your feet get dirty?

Has anyone ever washed your feet?

How does Jesus washing feet show that we should serve other people?

JUDAS

Jesus knew Judas planned to hurt Him.

Do you ever hurt a friend? On purpose?
If so, ask for forgiveness.

Is hiding your faith like turning away from Jesus or not being His friend?

Travel Time

Let's go back in the time tunnel to Isaiah 53:7. *Pow, pow, pow!* Isaiah wrote that Jesus would be the new lamb, the new sacrifice, to save us. The lamb was for Passover, to help Jews to remember that God had delivered them from slavery.

Chat about how Jesus gave us something more lasting than Passover.

Isaiah 53:7 He was oppressed and afflicted, yet he did not open his mouth; he was led like a lamb to the slaughter, and as a sheep before her shearers is silent, so he did not open his mouth.

Journal Time

Draw or write about the Last Supper.

Prayer Time

Dear Lord Jesus, thank You for giving us this special celebration of bread. Help us to not turn away from You. Help us tell others about You. Amen.

41 Peter's Denial

Bible Time

Matthew 26:14-16, 31-35, 47-56, 69-75; Mark 14:27-31, 43-50;
Luke 22:1-6, 31-35, 47-62; John 13:26-38, 18:1-18, 25-27

The leaders of God's people wanted Jesus dead.

Judas went to them and asked, "What will you give me for handing Jesus over to you?"

They gave Judas thirty pieces of silver, the price of a slave. Judas waited for a time when Jesus was almost alone.

Jesus and His disciples went to a garden.

"My children," Jesus said, "I will not be here much longer."

"Where will you go?" Peter asked.

"You cannot follow me there," Jesus answered.

"Why not?" Peter asked.

"This very night," Jesus said, "you will all turn away from me. But, after I have risen, I will go ahead of you to Galilee."

Peter said, "I will never turn away!"

"Simon, Simon," Jesus said to Peter, "Satan has asked to sift you like wheat [like sifting sand]. But I have prayed for you, that your faith may not fail. When you turn back to Me, help your brothers."

"Lord," cried Peter, "I am ready to go to prison and to die for You!"

"Peter," Jesus said, "this very night, before a rooster crows, three times you will say you don't even know Me."

"Even if I must die," cried Peter, "I will never deny You!"

The other disciples said the same thing.

Judas marched in. A crowd, armed with swords, followed. Judas had told the men to arrest the man he kissed.

Judas walked up to Jesus and said, "Hello, Teacher!"

Jesus said, "Friend, will you betray Me with a kiss? Do it quickly."

Judas kissed Jesus.

The disciples saw what might happen. One yelled, "Lord, should we use our swords?" Peter pulled out his sword. *Swish!* He cut off the ear of the high priest's servant.

"No!" Jesus yelled. "Put away your swords." He touched the man's head and healed his ear.

Then Jesus said, "You didn't arrest Me when I taught in the temple courts. This is taking place to fulfill the scriptures."

The disciples ran away. They all left Jesus.

Hi there!

Peter here again. I had problems with saying the right things at the right times. Today you'll learn about how what I said hurt Jesus.

- *Find out what friend of Jesus said, "I don't even know Him."*
- *Discover what the priests gave Judas.*

Then soldiers arrested Jesus and took Him to the high priest's house.

Peter followed them. People sat around a fire in the courtyard. Peter sat there, too.

A servant girl stared at Peter in the glow of the firelight, looking up and down. She pointed and said, "This man was with Him!"

Peter shook his head. "Woman, I don't know Him."

A little later, someone else stared at Peter, then said, "You're one of them!"

"Man," Peter yelled, "I am not!"

Tick, tock, an hour passed. Another person looked at Peter carefully. He yelled, "I'm sure this man was with Jesus. He's a Galilean."

"Man," screamed Peter, "I don't know what you're talking about!"

"Cock-a-doodle-doo!" a rooster crowed.

Peter remembered Jesus' words. He ran outside and cried.

Chat Time

Chat Word: *Courage* means to be brave or bold.
Chat about how Peter was afraid and did not have courage to say he knew Jesus.

COURAGE

Have you ever been afraid?

Have you ever had courage to do something even though you felt afraid?

What helps you be bold, so you tell people about Jesus and the Bible?

BETRAYAL

Judas acted like a friend and then turned away, or betrayed Jesus.

Did you ever have a friend who turned against you? What did you do?

Chat about how a lie hurts people.

WHAT JESUS KNEW

Chat about how Jesus knew about the rooster and Peter's denial.

Do you think it helped that Jesus said He knew about Peter's denial?

Do you think it helped Peter to know Jesus had prayed for him?

What else did Jesus say that might have given Peter hope?

WHAT HAPPENED WITH PETER

Peter said he would never deny Christ, so why did he?

Do you think Peter really believed he wouldn't deny Christ?

Have you ever made a promise you couldn't keep later?

Did you ever get so scared?

170

Travel Time

Let's go back in the time tunnel to Zechariah 11:12. *Pow, pow, pow!* The prophet Zechariah told about the payment to Judas hundreds of years before it happened.

Chat about how the Bible gave such true facts so long before things happened.

Zechariah 11:12 I told them, "If you think it best, give me my pay; but if not, keep it." So they paid me thirty pieces of silver.

Journal Time

Draw or write about Peter hearing the rooster crow.

Prayer Time

Lord, help us be bold and have courage to tell others about You. Thank You for always being with us so we don't have to be afraid. Amen.

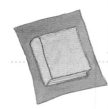

Bible Time Matthew 26:57-67, 27:1-26; Mark 14:53-65, 15:1-15; Luke 22:66-23:25; John 18:19-24, 28-40, 19:1-16

Soldiers took Jesus to Annas, a Jewish leader. Annas questioned Jesus about His teachings.

"Anyone could listen to Me," Jesus answered. "Nothing was secret. Ask people who listened, for they know what I said."

A Jewish soldier slapped Jesus, yelling, "Is that any way to answer?"

"If I said something wrong," Jesus said, "tell me what. Why hit Me for telling the truth?"

Then Annas sent Jesus, still tied up, to Caiaphas, the high priest. Teachers of Jewish laws and other priests crowded around. They hoped to find false facts so they could put Jesus to death. Many people told lies, but they gave different stories. The priests couldn't use that information.

One person said, "He said, 'I will destroy this temple made by men and in three days I will build a new one, not made by man.'" People disagreed about that, too.

Caiaphas asked Jesus, "What do you have to say?"

Jesus didn't speak.

The high priest demanded, "Under the living God, are You the Messiah, the Son of God?"

"Yes," Jesus answered. "In the future the Son of Man will sit at the right hand of God and ride on clouds."

The high priest asked, "Did you hear Him?"

The people cried, "He is worthy of death." They spit in His face, pounded Him with their fists, and slapped Him.

Before sunrise, they took Jesus to Pilate. Pilate was not a Jew, but he was in charge of Jerusalem.

Pilate asked, "What is this man's crime?"

They cried, "He leads people to be bad. He tells them not to pay taxes. He says He is a king."

Pilate said, "Then punish Him with your laws."

They yelled, "We cannot kill anyone!" Only Romans had that power.

So Pilate asked Jesus, "Are you king of the Jews?"

"Yes," Jesus said. He also said, "My kingdom is in a different world. I came into this world to tell the truth."

This scared Pilate. Since Jesus was from Galilee, Pilate sent Him to King Herod, the leader of Galilee.

Herod asked Jesus many questions and hoped to see a miracle. Jesus stayed silent. At last, Herod sent Jesus back to Pilate.

Pilate's wife sent a message. "I had a bad dream about Jesus. Don't hurt Him."

This scared Pilate more so he had men beat Jesus. Every year Pilate let one person go free from jail. He asked the people, "Do you want Jesus freed?"

The people yelled, "No! Let Barabbas go." So, Pilate let Barabbas, a very wicked man, go free.

Pilate asked, "What about Jesus?"

"Kill Him, crucify Him!" the people yelled.

Finally Pilate washed his hands and said, "I will have nothing to do with Jesus."

"Okay, blame us," cried the people.

Pilate let them take Jesus to kill Him.

Chat Time

Chat Word: *Accuse* means to say someone did something wrong.
Chat about how the priests and people accused Jesus of crimes.

ANGER

People hit Jesus because they were angry. Is that a good reason?

LIES

The priests wanted Jesus dead even if it meant telling lies. Chat about that.
Have you ever told a lie? Why?
Has anyone ever accused you or told a lie about you? How did it feel?
What is truth?

What can you do when you feel so angry you want to hurt someone?
When you are angry, try one of these: pray, take deep breaths, talk to an adult, think through the problem, or hold your hands together.
Chat about more ways to calm down when you are angry.

TRIALS

A trial is when people listen then decide if someone broke a law. Talk about trials, the courts, and judges in your country.

COURT

Do you listen to both sides when something wrong happens? When Pilate heard Jesus came to tell the truth, why did it scare him?

Did you ever accuse someone then find out they didn't do it?

Travel Time

Let's go back in the time tunnel to Isaiah 50:6 and 53:7. *Pow, pow, pow!* The prophet said Jesus would stay silent, and people would beat Jesus, and that's what happened!

Chat about how Jesus did not fight when enemies hurt Him.

Isaiah 50:6 I offered my back to those who beat me, my cheeks to those who pulled out my beard; I did not hide my face from mocking and spitting.

Isaiah 53:7 He was oppressed and afflicted, yet he did not open his mouth; he was led like a lamb to the slaughter, and as a sheep before her shearers is silent, so he did not open his mouth.

Journal Time

Draw or write about Jesus and His trial.

Prayer Time

Jesus, You told the truth when people lied. It hurt You so much. You did it because You love us. Thank You. Help us always tell the truth. Amen.

43 Jesus Dies

Bible Time Matthew 27:27-61; Mark 15:16-47; Luke 23:26-56; John 19:16-42

Soldiers pulled off Jesus' clothes then put a purple robe on Him. They placed a crown made of thorns on His head. They teased Him, "Hail, King of the Jews!" *Whack!* Soldiers bashed Jesus on the head, beat Him, and spit on Him. They pulled off the purple robe, put His clothes back on, and led Him to be crucified. Jesus carried the heavy cross, dragging it toward Skull Hill, also called Golgotha. The soldiers grabbed a man named Simon and forced him to carry the cross.

Many people followed. Women cried. Jesus looked at the women and said, "Don't cry for me. Cry for your children and what will happen in bad times."

Bang! Bang! At nine in the morning, on Skull Hill, soldiers took off Jesus' coat and outer clothes then nailed Him to the cross. They also crucified two robbers, one on each side of Jesus. Four soldiers divided the clothes and threw dice to choose who would keep the coat.

People mixed wine with something bitter to let Jesus drink. He tasted it but would not drink it.

Pilate had a sign made that said "Jesus of Nazareth, King of the Jews." The soldiers hammered it onto the cross. It was written in three languages. The chief priests complained, "Write that He claimed to be king."

"What I have written I have written," replied Pilate.

People yelled, "Come off the cross

Hello,

John here again! Today is the saddest but one of the best stories you'll ever hear. You will learn about what Jesus did for you.

- *Find out what was written and put on the cross.*
- *Discover who stayed by Jesus as He died.*

and save Yourself!"

"Father," Jesus cried, "forgive them. They don't know what they are doing."

One robber teased Jesus. The other asked the first robber, "Don't you fear God? We were bad, but this man did no wrong."

That robber said to Jesus, "Remember me when You enter Your kingdom."

"Truly," Jesus said, "today you will be with me in paradise."

About noon the sky darkened. Darkness covered the land for three hours. Friends of Jesus stood by, including Mary His mother, His aunt Mary, Mary Magdalene, and a disciple Jesus loved.

"Dear woman," Jesus said to His mother, "here is your son," meaning the disciple, and to the disciple He said, "Here is your mother." After that, the disciple took Mary into his own home.

"I thirst," Jesus called.

Someone soaked a sponge in a jar of wine vinegar and placed it against His mouth.

Jesus drank then said, "It is finished. Father, I give You my spirit." He bowed His head and died. The earth shook, the temple curtain tore in half, graves opened up, and dead people who were holy came back to life.

A soldier pierced Jesus' side. Blood and water flowed out. Joseph, a Jewish leader, took Jesus' body, placed it in a tomb, and rolled a large rock over the opening.

Chat Time

Chat Word: *Crucify* means to nail someone to a cross made of wood and to let him hang on it until dead.

LOVE

Chat about how Jesus said a friend would be willing to die for His friends.
Chat about why Jesus died.

How does that show Jesus loves you?

Chat about how painful it must have been to have nails in Jesus' hands and feet and hang on a cross.

TEASING

How did people tease Jesus?

Does teasing and spitting on someone hurt him?

What can you do when you see someone teasing another person?

WHEN JESUS DIED

Chat about what happened when Jesus died.

Why did Jesus ask God, the Father, to forgive those who crucified Him?

Chat about how the curtain kept people away from the most holy place. Does anything keep us from God now?

THE CROSS

Chat about what the cross means to you.
Chat about how Adam and Eve's sin was about a tree.

Travel Time

Let's go back in the time tunnel to Zechariah 12:10. *Pow, pow, pow!* Long before Christ's death the prophets spoke about how Jesus would die and be pierced.
Chat about what it means to mourn.

Zechariah 12:10 "And I will pour out on the house of David and the inhabitants of Jerusalem a spirit of grace and supplication. They will look on me, the one they have pierced, and they will mourn for him as one mourns for an only child, and grieve bitterly for him as one grieves for a firstborn son."

Journal Time

Draw or write about what the cross means to you.

Forgiveness

Love

Living forever with Jesus

Prayer Time

Thank You, Jesus, for dying so that we might live forever. Help us forgive everyone no matter how much they hurt us. Amen.

44 The Resurrection

Bible Time Matthew 27:57-28:15; Mark 15:42-16:8;
Luke 23:50-24:11; John 19:38-20:18

The day after Jesus died, the Jewish leaders went to Pilate and said, "Jesus told people He would come back to life after three days. So, give orders to have the tomb guarded and kept closed until the third day. His disciples might come and steal His body and tell people He is alive. This would be the worst trick."

Pilate sent guards, and they sealed the stone in front of the tomb.

On the third day, as the sun rose, the earth shook. An angel of the Lord came from heaven, rolled back the stone, and sat on it. The angel wore dazzling clothes, like lightning.

The angel scared the guards so much that they fell down like dead men.

Mary Magdalene, Mary, the mother of James, Joanna, and Salome carried spices to the tomb. They planned to anoint Jesus' body.

When they came near, they saw the stone was already rolled away. They rushed inside but did not see Jesus. Suddenly two men, in clothes as bright as lightning, stood beside them.

"Do not fear," the men said. "You are searching for Jesus, but why look for the living among the dead? He is risen. Remember how He said, 'The Son of Man must be crucified and will be raised again on the third day.'"

The men added, "Go, tell Peter and the disciples, 'He is going to Galilee as He promised.'"

Shaking and confused, the women ran away. Mary Magdalene found Simon Peter and John, the disciple whom Jesus loved. Mary cried, "They took the Lord from the

Praise the Lord today!

My name is Mary Magdalene, and Jesus changed my life by casting seven demons out of me! Today you'll find out what happened three days after Jesus died.

- *Find out why Jesus did not want Mary to touch Him.*
- *Discover who saw Jesus first after He came back to life.*

180

tomb! We don't know where they put Him!"

John and Peter ran to the tomb. John ran faster but did not go inside the tomb. He waited for Peter. Peter reached the tomb and ran right inside. He saw the cloth that had been wrapped around Jesus. He also saw the cloth that had been around Jesus' head, all rolled up. At last John went inside the tomb. Then they both believed but did not understand. They each walked home.

Mary Magdalene returned to the grave. Tears rolled down her cheeks.

"Why do you cry?" the angels asked.

"They took my Lord away, and I don't know where they put Him." She turned around and saw Jesus, but she did not know Him. She thought He was the gardener.

He said, "Woman, why are you crying?"

"Please," Mary said, "tell me where you put Him."

"Mary," Jesus called.

"Teacher!" Mary shouted happily.

"Don't touch Me," Jesus told her, "for I haven't seen the Father yet. Go, tell the brothers, 'I am going to our Father, our God.'"

Mary ran and told them, "I saw the Lord!"

Chat Time

Chat Word: *Resurrection* means to come back to life after dying.
Chat about how all believers who die will be resurrected.

THE GUARDS
What made the guards fall down?

Why were the Jewish leaders worried?
Do you think they wanted Jesus to come back to life? Why?

KNOWING JESUS
Why do you think Mary Magdalene didn't know Jesus when she saw Him?

Why do you think some people have trouble believing in Jesus?

How does reading the Bible help you to know truth?

NEW LIFE
Do you think Jesus looked different when He came back to life?
Chat about how we know we will be raised to new life.

Travel Time

Let's go back in the time tunnel to Psalm 49:15. *Pow, pow, pow!* Wow! The psalm praises God for raising Jesus from the grave. ***Chat about how Jesus did all that was written about His resurrection in the Old Testament.***

Psalm 49:15 But God will redeem my soul from the grave; he will surely take me to himself.

Journal Time

Write or draw about Jesus rising from the dead.

Prayer Time

Thank You, Jesus, for doing all the scriptures promised. We rejoice that You have risen. Help us share our joy with others. Amen.

45 The Ascension

Bible Time Matthew 28:11-20; Mark 16:1-20; Luke 24:13-53; John 20:19–21:24; Acts 1:1-11

hen the soldiers woke up and saw the empty tomb, they found the Jewish leaders and told them what happened. Oh, no! The leaders paid the soldiers lots of money to lie and say friends of Jesus stole His body during the night. To this day, many people believe the lie.

Many people saw Jesus after He rose. The other women who were with Mary Magdalene saw Him and touched His feet.

Two friends walked with Jesus on the road to Emmaus but did not realize He was the Lord. They told Him they were sad because Jesus, a powerful prophet, had died. They also said angels had told the women Jesus was alive. Jesus walked with them and explained the scriptures.

At last, they stopped and Jesus broke bread with them. Then they knew Him but then He disappeared. They rushed back to

Jerusalem to tell others what happened. The two friends found the disciples and told them about seeing Jesus.

Poof! Suddenly, Jesus appeared and said, "Peace be with you." He showed them the nail wounds in His hands and feet and invited them to touch the wounds. He also ate bread while they watched.

The disciple Thomas was not there and did not believe they saw Jesus alive. Thomas said, "Unless I put my finger in the place where the nails were in His hands and the wound on His side, I will not believe."

Eight days later, Jesus appeared to the disciples again. He held out His hands to Thomas, "Thomas, touch My wounds."

Thomas believed, but Jesus said, "Blessed are those who do not see but believe."

The next forty days after Jesus rose, many people saw and listened to Jesus. The disciples even had a picnic on the beach with Jesus. After the picnic, Jesus spoke with Peter, who told people three times he didn't know Jesus.

So, three times Jesus asked Peter, "Do you love Me?"

Each time, Peter answered, "You know I love You."

"Feed My lambs!" Jesus replied each time.

Jesus told all His disciples, "Go and make disciples in all countries, baptizing people in the name of the Father, the Son, and the Holy Spirit." Jesus promised the Father would give them power. Wow!

Jesus said, "Do not leave Jerusalem until you receive the gift from My Father. In a few days you will be baptized with the Holy Spirit."

They watched as Jesus rose. Up! Up! Up! into the heavens, until a cloud hid Him. The disciples stared at the sky. Suddenly two men, dressed in white, stood beside them.

The men said, "Jesus, who has been taken into heaven, will come back the same way."

Hi there!
It's Mary again. I have more news for you today about what happened after Jesus rose. It's such good news!

- *Find out who wanted to touch the wounds of Jesus.*
- *Discover what Jesus told the disciples to do.*

Chat Time

Chat Word: *Ascension* means to rise to a higher place.

Chat about the Ascension and promise of Christ's return.

THE GREAT COMMISSION

Talk about how Jesus' command to make disciples and baptize is called the Great Commission.

Are you helping to carry out that command?

Who can you tell about Jesus today?

THE LIE

Why do you think the Jewish leaders wanted to hide the truth about Jesus?

Chat about why some people don't want to believe in Jesus.

What helps you believe?

JESUS AFTER HE ROSE

Do you think Jesus looked different after He rose?

Why did some people not know Jesus when they saw Him?

How did Jesus get in rooms without opening doors?

THE ASCENSION

Why do you think the disciples stared after Jesus went behind clouds?

What did Jesus promise would happen after He left?

Chat about the Holy Spirit and the power of the Holy Spirit.

Chat about how Jesus will come back.

Travel Time

Let's go back in the time tunnel to Psalm 68:18. *Pow, pow, pow!* The prophets spoke about how Jesus would not stay dead and buried. **Chat about how believers will not stay dead.**

Psalm 68:18 When you ascended on high, you led captives in your train; you received gifts from men, even from the rebellious–that you, O Lord God, might dwell there.

Journal Time

Draw or write about when you will see Jesus come back.

Prayer Time

Thank You, Father, for taking Jesus to heaven and the promise of Your Holy Spirit. Help us be good disciples. Help us tell others about Jesus. Amen.

46 Pentecost – the Church Begins

Bible Time Acts 2:1-47, 20:16

The day of Pentecost came fifty days after Jesus' resurrection. Pentecost means fifty. Long ago, God told His people to celebrate this day, also called the Feast of Weeks, to celebrate the wheat harvest. People gave God the first grain picked.

The disciples, Mary, and others had been waiting in Jerusalem for what Christ had promised, the sending of the Holy Spirit.

Whoosh! A strong and powerful wind from heaven swirled in the house. *Whoosh!* The wind filled the house. They saw something like tongues of fire that pulled apart and rested on each person.

Strange noises filled the house as these believers spoke in other languages. Even people outside heard. Many people were in Jerusalem for Pentecost. A crowd gathered outside the house. People listened in surprise. They each heard someone speaking in their own language. The Holy Spirit had filled each person.

Someone said, "How can this happen? All the men in the house are Galileans, but we each hear in our own language. They speak to people from strange places like Parthia, Medea, Elam, Mesopotamia, Judea, and even Asia!"

"They must have drunk too much wine," others yelled.

Hi again from me, Peter!

May you be filled with God's Holy Spirit as you read how the Christian church began. I was there, and it is an exciting story!

- *Find out what rested over the head of each disciple.*
- *Discover how many people were baptized on the day of Pentecost.*

Peter stood up with the other disciples. He spoke loudly so all could hear.

"Listen," Peter called, "it's early in the morning. No one is drunk. What you hear was prophesied by Joel. He said, 'God will pour out His Spirit. Young people will see visions, and old men will have dreams. God will show wonders from heaven. And everyone who calls on the name of the Lord will be saved.'"

Peter told the crowd about Jesus and how after He died on the cross God brought Him back to life. He reminded the people that David had said God would not let the Holy One stay dead.

Peter also said, "Jesus is Lord and Christ."

The words touched people's hearts and they asked, "What should we do?"

"Repent and be baptized in the name of Jesus Christ," came Peter's answer. "He forgives sins. You will receive the gift of the Holy Spirit. The promise is for you and for your children and for all who call on God."

They baptized everyone who believed, about three thousand people! These new believers followed the disciples' teachings. They called the disciples "apostles," which means "messengers."

The apostles did many miracles and wonders. The believers sold what they owned and lived together, sharing everything. They met daily in the temple courts. They broke bread in their homes and ate together with great joy. God added to their number every day. The church spread to other cities and towns.

In the city named Antioch, people started calling the believers Christians. Pentecost remained a special day that early Christians celebrated every year.

Chat Time

PENTECOST

How many people were baptized on Pentecost?

Chat about how your church celebrates Pentecost.

Chat Word: The *Holy Spirit* is another person of God. He is called the helper by Jesus and is here to help believers understand the word of God. He also gives us special gifts such as healing and teaching.

Chat about how the Holy Spirit can help you.

Jesus wants us to harvest souls, so chat about how to do that.

PROMISE FOR ALL

Peter said the Holy Spirit is for all people who do what?

Talk about the gifts of the Holy Spirit. Look them up in Romans 12 and 1 Corinthians 12. Talk about the fruits of the Spirit. Look up those in Galatians 5:22.

ONE SPARK

Disciples saw little flames rest above their heads. What can happen with a little flame or spark? with the power of the Holy Spirit?

How can you spread your joy or burning love for God to others?

Travel Time

Let's go back in the time tunnel to Joel 2:28-32 and John 14:1, 26. *Pow, pow, pow!* Prophets and Jesus told people that God would pour out His Spirit on all believers.

Chat about how the Holy Spirit, whom Jesus called the helper, does help us.

Joel 2:28 "And afterward, I will pour out my Spirit on all people. Your sons and daughters will prophesy, your old men will dream dreams, your young men will see visions."

John 14:26 "But the Counselor, the Holy Spirit, whom the Father will send in my name, will teach you all things and will remind you of everything I have said to you."

Journal Time

Draw or write about Pentecost.

Prayer Time

Thank You, Father, for sending the Holy Spirit. Help us be filled with the Spirit and have the power to bring others to belief in Jesus. Amen.

47 Paul's Conversion

Zip! Whiz! Smack!
Rocks flew in the air and hit Stephen. Angry people kept throwing more stones. Stephen fell on his knees.

"Lord," Stephen cried, "do not hold this sin against them." At this, he fell asleep.

Saul, a Pharisee, watched and approved of people killing Stephen, a good man who had believed in Jesus and preached about Him. Saul hurt many believers and put many in prison.

Saul asked the high priest for letters to imprison believers in the city of Damascus. Once he had the letters, Saul rode toward Damascus with men to help him.

Zap! Flash! Light from heaven, brighter than the sun, dazzled him. Saul fell to the ground.

"Saul! Saul!" a voice from heaven boomed. "Why are you hurting Me?"

"Who are You, Lord?" Saul cried.

"I am Jesus. You are hurting me!" the voice called. "Rise and go into Damascus. There you will be told the plans I have for you."

Paul stood up. Blink! Blink! He could not see although his eyes were open. The men with Paul saw the light and heard the voice, too. They led him into the city. For three days Saul stayed blind.

Now Ananias, a disciple in Damascus, saw a vision in which the Lord called him. "Here I am, Lord," Ananias answered. The Lord sent Ananias to lay hands on Saul.

Saul also had a vision that a man named Ananias would lay hands on him and restore his sight.

Ananias felt scared and exclaimed, "This man harmed many believers in Jerusalem, Lord!"

The Lord said, "I have chosen him to tell the

Grace and peace be with you.

I'm Paul, and that's how I greeted people in my letters! Today you'll find out how I became a Christian and God changed my name from Saul to Paul.

- *Find out how Paul lost and regained his eyesight.*
- *Discover what Paul did before he became a Christian.*

Gentiles [that is, people who are not Jews], kings, and Jews about Me."

Ananias obeyed. When he laid hands on Paul, he said, "Brother Saul, the Lord Jesus, who spoke to you on the road, sent me so you will see again and be filled with the Holy Spirit."

At once, thin coverings, like scales on a fish, fell from Saul's eyes. Saul could see again! He was baptized, then he ate and felt stronger.

Right away, Saul began telling others that Jesus is God's Son. This surprised people. They knew he had troubled followers of Jesus. But Saul kept teaching about Jesus and became better at it.

The Jews planned to kill Saul when he left Damascus, but Saul found out about their plan. Friends took Saul to the city wall and put him in a huge basket. They pushed the basket through a hole in the wall and lowered it to the ground. Saul climbed out and went to Jerusalem. Believers started calling him Paul. He spent the rest of his life teaching and writing about Jesus.

Chat Time

Chat Word: *Convert* means to change your faith and turn to God from sin.
Chat about someone you know who converted.

CHANGING
What made Paul change and stop hurting believers?

Do you need to change any bad behavior? Who can help you change?
Is your heart turned to God? If not, pray and tell Jesus you believe in Him.

FOLLOWING CHRIST
What did Paul do right after he was baptized?

Do you spend time telling people about Jesus?

Think of one person who needs Jesus and plan to tell them about Jesus.

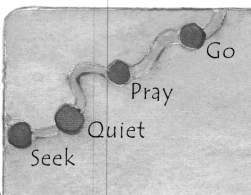

Go
Pray
Quiet
Seek

GOD'S PLANS
What plans did God have for Paul?

Are you ready for anything God wants you to do?
Read Psalm 139 and you'll see God has plans for you, too!
Pray and ask God to show you His plans for your life.

Travel Time

Let's go back in the time tunnel to Matthew 28:19-20. *Pow, pow, pow!* That's when Jesus told the disciples to tell everyone about Him. ***Chat about how Jesus is always with each believer.***

Matthew 28:19 "Therefore go and make disciples of all nations, baptizing them in the name of the Father and of the Son and of the Holy Spirit, and teaching them to obey everything I have commanded you. And surely I am with you always, to the very end of the age."

Journal Time

Write or draw about you telling someone about Jesus.

Prayer Time

Lord, You are so great and can change the hearts of all people. Show us Your plans and give us the strength to follow You and tell others about You. Amen.

48 Peter's Vision

Peter kept telling people about Jesus and performed many miracles.

Peter healed Aeneas, a man who had not walked for eight years.

Two men begged Peter to go to Joppa and heal a woman named Dorcas. When Peter came to Joppa, Dorcas had already died. Women cried and showed Peter clothes she had sewn for them.

Peter sent the women out. He knelt, prayed, then said, "Dorcas, get up!" She sat up!

People who saw these miracles believed in Jesus.

Cornelius, a Roman officer, lived in Caesarea. He was a Gentile, meaning he was not a Jew, but he prayed and gave a lot to the poor. One day he saw an angel in a vision, or picture in his mind. It scared him, and he asked, "What is it?"

The angel said, "God knows about your prayers and gifts to the poor. Ask Peter, who is in Joppa, to come visit." Cornelius sent three men to find Peter.

In Joppa the next day, Peter went on the roof to pray. Peter saw a vision, too. He saw the sky open and a sheet come down, filled with all sorts of animals.

A voice said, "Peter, eat these animals."

196

"No, Lord," Peter said, "Jewish laws do not allow me to eat them."

The voice called, "If God says it is good, then don't disagree."

Peter saw the same vision three times. Then the Holy Spirit said, "Three men are searching for you. Go with them, for I sent them."

Peter and other believers went with the men. Cornelius had invited many friends to his home to hear about God. Cornelius bowed when Peter walked in.

Peter pulled Cornelius up, saying, "Don't bow to me. I'm just a person." Then he said, "You know it's against Jewish law for me to enter a Gentile's house, but God sent me."

Cornelius told Peter about his vision and said, "We are waiting to hear God's message."

Peter told the people about God, how Jesus died for them and came back to life. He said, "God does not love one person more than another. He loves all people, from all nations. He forgives sins."

As Peter spoke, the Holy Spirit came upon everyone. They spoke in other languages. They praised God. This surprised the believers with Peter.

Peter said, "How can we not baptize them? They were sent the Holy Spirit, too." So, they baptized everyone.

The other apostles heard and wondered about Peter visiting Cornelius and his Gentile friends. Peter told them of his vision and how God sent the Holy Spirit.

The apostles praised God and said, "God gave even the Gentiles forgiveness and eternal life!"

It's me, Peter,
and I want you to know God loves you! Today you'll learn how God used me to tell others about Him and how God taught me a lesson.

- *Find out what Peter saw in his vision.*
- *Discover what the Holy Spirit did for Cornelius.*

Chat Time

Chat Word: *Witness* means to tell the truth about what you know is real.
Chat about how Peter was a witness for Christ.

VISIONS

Chat about the visions of Peter and Cornelius.

What would you think if you had a vision?

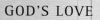

GOD'S LOVE

Does God love you as much as anyone else?

Do you know someone who needs to hear about God's love?

BEING A WITNESS

What do you know about Jesus? Is that enough to tell someone else?

Who can you witness to and when?

Practice witnessing to people in your family.

Travel Time

Let's go back in the time tunnel to Isaiah 42:6. *Pow, pow, pow!* The prophets told how God wanted His people to bring His message to all people.

Chat about how God wants you to be a light.

Isaiah 49:6 "...I will also make you a light for the Gentiles, that you may bring salvation to the ends of the earth."

Journal Time

Write or draw about Peter's vision.

Prayer Time

Thank You, Jesus, for loving every person, including each of us! Help us learn more about You and share what we know with others. Amen.

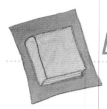

Bible Time Acts 27; 2 Corinthians 11

Peace to you from me, Paul.

I was called by God to be a Christian leader. Today you'll learn about a time a storm caused problems for me.

- *Find out how people tried to stop Paul from witnessing.*
- *Discover what broke the boat that carried Paul.*

Nothing stopped Paul from telling people about Jesus. This made Jewish and Roman leaders angry. The Jewish leaders feared people would no longer listen to them. The Roman leaders feared they would not pay taxes or serve the Roman rulers.

They tried to stop Paul. *Smack!* Men beat Paul. *Clang! clang!* Men chained Paul and locked him in prison. They whipped him. Men even dragged Paul out of town and stoned him, then left him when they thought he had died.

That didn't stop Paul! He rose up from the stoning, sang in prison, and told people who hurt him about Jesus. Paul knew how to feel happy in good or bad times because he trusted God all the time.

Governor Felix kept Paul in prison near Jerusalem for two years. Then Festus became the new governor. King Agrippa visited Festus, heard about Paul, and asked to meet Paul. Paul told Agrippa and Festus about Jesus. Festus thought Paul was crazy to talk about someone dying and coming back to life. But, the men agreed that Paul had done nothing wrong. They chose to send Paul to Rome, in Italy, to be tried by Caesar.

What a long trip for Paul to go across the sea to Rome! First, Paul and other prisoners sailed on a boat to Lycia. Then Paul sailed on another ship toward Italy.

It was almost winter and dangerous to sail at that time of year. Paul said the journey would end with the ship sinking. The captain sailed anyway.

Whoosh! A storm called a "northeaster" caught the ship. They could not sail against the strong winds. The storm tossed the boat around.

Smack! The huge waves hurt the boat. The men tied ropes around the boat to hold it together. The wind kept blowing. They didn't see the sun or any stars for days and days. The sailors thought they would all die.

But Paul knew better. "Be brave. Last night an angel from God came to me. The angel said, 'The people on the boat will live.'" Paul added, "We'll crash on an island."

The ship was tossed closer to land. One morning Paul told everyone to eat. After Paul ate, they also ate. Everyone felt better.

They tried to sail to the shore. Crash, the boat hit a sandbar. *Boom! Crash!* Waves broke the ship into pieces. The army captain, who guarded Paul and the prisoners, told those who could swim to jump into the sea and swim. He told the other people to hold onto boards and float to shore. Hooray! All 276 people landed safely.

Later Paul went to Rome and told more people about Jesus, even the leader of the Roman empire.

Chat Time

Chat Word: *Content* means to be happy or satisfied whether good things or bad things happen.

TRUSTING GOD

Have you, like Paul, had bad things happen?

How has God helped you in the past with your problems?

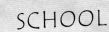

DOING GOD'S WILL

Why did Paul keep telling others about Jesus even when men hurt him?

Chat about how Paul said God called him to tell people about Jesus.

BEING CONTENT

Do you know how to be happy in good times and in bad?

Can you enjoy a game whether you win or lose?

What do you think God wants you to do with your life?

Talk about how it can be hard to trust God when things seem to go wrong.

Travel Time

Let's go back in the time tunnel to John 16:33. *Pow, pow, pow!* Jesus told us we could have peace. **Chat about how Jesus overcame the world.**

John 16:33 "I have told you these things, so that in me you may have peace. In this world you will have trouble. But take heart! I have overcome the world."

Journal Time

Draw or write about a time you trusted God.

Prayer Time

God, You are so great! You care for us and protect us. Help us trust in You and be patient when we wait for Your answers. Amen.

50 Revelation

Bible Time Revelation

"Write what you see and hear," a voice called to John. John looked and saw seven lamps and someone like the Son of Man with eyes like fire. His voice sounded like a waterfall. He held seven stars in His right hand. John fell down at His feet.

The man touched John and said, "Don't be afraid. I was dead and am alive. Write what you see. It will take place later. The seven stars are the angels of seven churches. The lamps are the seven churches."

John wrote messages to the seven churches that the man gave him. Then John looked and saw an open door to heaven.

The voice said, "Come, see what will happen." John saw someone sitting on the King's throne in heaven. A glowing rainbow surrounded the throne.

Four strange beasts sang, "Holy! Holy! Holy! He will live forever."

John saw the Lamb who had been killed take a paper with seven seals from the King. Each seal He opened brought something terrible to earth. When Jesus, the Lamb, opened the sixth seal, the earth shook, the sun

Hello, dear friends.
It's John, the apostle Jesus loved. Have you ever wondered about the future? Well, God showed me pictures in my mind about the future. That's what you'll learn about today!

- *Find out what was around God's throne in heaven.*
- *Discover what John saw in his vision.*

turned black, the moon turned red as blood, and stars fell from the sky. Mountains were pushed out of place. People hid in caves. People died from hunger and polluted water. Locusts ate the plants of the earth. Fire, smoke, and yellow acid killed people.

A war broke out in heaven against a dragon. The dragon lost. He is the old snake called Satan.

Then a beast and a lying prophet ruled earth and made people worship the beast. The dragon gave them great power. For more than three years this beast ruled earth.

Then, John saw Jesus come on a cloud and stand on Mount Zion. A great many people stood with Him. From heaven John heard sounds of roaring water, thunder, and people playing harps.

Angels poured out bowls of God's anger. Sores fell on people who worshiped the beast. The sea turned to blood, the sun turned so hot it burned people, and the place where the beast ruled turned dark.

An angel poured out the last bowl of anger. *Flash! Boom! Crash!* Lightning flashed, thunder roared, and the earth shook. Cities and mountains everywhere crashed.

God and His army caught the beast and the lying prophet and threw them into the lake of fire. An angel chained the dragon and threw him into the bottomless pit. Then God judged the people.

Finally, John saw a new earth and new heaven. John saw a new and beautiful holy city come down from heaven.

A voice called, "Now God will live with His people."

Jesus said, "I am coming soon."

Come, Lord Jesus!

Chat Time

Chat Word: *Revelation* means to show or tell someone the future.

DISASTERS AND GOD'S ANGER

Why do you think God will pour out anger on the earth?

Chat about how God gave John this revelation of the future.

THE NEW EARTH

What do you think God will do differently when He makes a new earth?

Chat about how the new holy city will come down from heaven.

THE DRAGON, BEAST, AND LYING PROPHET

Why do you think the Bible says the dragon, or snake, is Satan?

How do you think these three evil beings will fool people?

Why do you think the lying prophet is called an Anti-Christ, which means against Christ?

Chat about a surprise in the holy city–a tree that will produce twelve kinds of fruit instead of only one type per tree.

Travel Time

Let's go back in the time tunnel to Isaiah 66:16. *Pow, pow, pow!* Isaiah told people that one day God would judge everyone.

Chat about how God will come again and will then judge people.

Isaiah 66:16 For with fire and with his sword the LORD will execute judgment upon all men, and many will be those slain by the LORD.

Journal Time

Write or draw about God's throne in heaven.

Prayer Time

Lord Jesus, come again soon. We are waiting for You! Amen.